CW00645712

CHILDREN IN RENEWAL

Children in Renewal

Alan Price

Hodder & Stoughton
LONDON SYDNEY AUCKLAND

Copyright © 1996 Alan Price

First published in Great Britain 1996

The right of Alan Price to be identified as the Author of
the Work has been asserted by him in accordance with the
Copyright, Designs and Patents Act 1988.

10 9 8 7 6 5 4 3 2 1

All rights reserved. No part of this publication may be
reproduced, stored in a retrieval system, or transmitted,
in any form or by any means without the prior written permission
of the publisher, nor be otherwise circulated in any form of binding
or cover other than that in which it is published and without a
similar condition being imposed on the subsequent purchaser.

British Library Cataloguing in Publication Data
A record for this book is available from the British Library

ISBN 0 340 65160 1

Typeset by CentraCet, Cambridge
Printed and bound in Great Britain by
Cox & Wyman Ltd, Reading, Berks

Hodder and Stoughton Ltd
A Division of Hodder Headline PLC
338 Euston Road
London NW1 3BH

Contents

Introduction

I was nothing extraordinary as a child. I was born in Waterloo, Liverpool, and baptised at the Church of England service of Evensong, at the church across the road where my parents were at that time regular members. However, I had a nominal Christian upbringing, which included Sunday School, a church-sponsored Boy Scout troop, membership in the church choir and confirmation at fourteen. I had always been 'religious', whilst not letting it interfere too much in my life. That changed in 1967 when, at the age of nineteen, I had a profound experience of Christ and the Holy Spirit that changed my life for ever. Eighteen months later, I had begun my training in the Church Army, having been called by God to be something different from a Christian office worker.

Even in those intervening months I had a vision for children's work, and I was involved in the radical reformation of my local church Sunday School. However, although I did a lot of work with children during my training and subsequent ministry, it was not until 1983 that I began to specialise in evangelism and ministry with children and young people.

Part of my conversion experience was an encounter with the Holy Spirit. I was hungry for the things of God, and sought fellowship and teaching wherever I could find them. One such place was a house church which met in the front room of a Victorian terraced house in Kirkdale, Liverpool 8. There I witnessed the outpouring of the gifts of the Holy

Spirit, with speaking in tongues, prophecy, healing and deliverance from evil spirits. These people had an even greater passion for Jesus; if the Holy Spirit could do that for them, then I wanted this experience too! So I joined those who were involved in what was termed 'Charismatic Renewal'. This was such a natural part of my early growth in faith that I was surprised to find the issue was a subject of controversy when I joined the Church Army!

Throughout my ministry as a Church Army evangelist I sought to preach and teach a 'whole' Gospel of repentance, faith in Christ and the receiving of the Holy Spirit. This was comparatively easy with adults and teenagers, and many not only came to faith but also experienced the power of the Spirit in their lives. However, despite my experience and my desire for children to enter this fullness, for years I failed to enable them make a similar connection. Knowing Jesus and receiving Him as a personal Friend was OK, but how could I help them to know the 'incomparably great power for us who believe' (Eph. 1:19)?

The real breakthrough came in 1989, when I was invited by Bishop David Pytches and Revd Barry Kissell of St Andrew's, Chorleywood, to lead the children's ministry (five- to eleven-year-olds) at New Wine, a family camp to be held at the Royal Bath and West Showground in Somerset. At that time I was on the staff of Christ Church, Chorleywood, and was leader of the Chorleywood Holiday Week, organised jointly by the local churches. This annual event drew over one thousand children from the surrounding area. The plan was simply to transplant the Holiday Week from Chorleywood and run it again on site at New Wine. However, Holiday Week was an evangelistic event, and it seemed that the clientele of New Wine would be Christians. The aim of the camp was clearly stated as 'teaching and ministry in the power of the Holy Spirit'. It was only a few weeks before the event that the planning team and I realised that God wanted the equivalent ministry for the children! There was no turning back. What I began to learn then in the 'Captain's Crew' (as the children's ministry was called) was the beginning of the most exciting adventure in ministry in my life.

It is well to define terms. When we talk of children, people have different ideas of the age group concerned. For many, it refers to those of pre-secondary school age. At that stage, children themselves generally prefer to be called 'young people'. However, some adults use the term to describe those who are sixteen years and under, who are still in full-time primary or secondary education. It is as well, therefore, to be clear that in this book I refer to the age group with which I have had most experience, primarily five- to eleven-year-olds.

Renewal is the other word that needs clarification. I mean charismatic renewal, that renewal of love for God and refreshment of faith in Christ that comes from a personal experience of the power of the Holy Spirit – traditionally referred to as the 'baptism in the Holy Spirit'. This is often accompanied by supernatural manifestations or gifts of the Holy Spirit (in particular as mentioned in 1 Corinthians 12:1–11). I would hasten to add here that I do not believe this to be necessarily a 'second experience' of God.

I am well aware that I am still very much a beginner, and there is much that I have still to learn. I do not claim to be an 'expert', or to have all the answers. However, I am pleased to offer the results of my discoveries and the methods I have used to help others embark on the adventure.

Captain Alan Price, C.A.

1

God's will and plan for children

We have a vision: an army of little children rising fearlessly from our midst. This is an army motivated by simple faith – and a personal friendship with the King of the Universe – Jesus Christ. He will empower and lead them in simple obedience to accomplish all of His purposes before His final return. Just as when He first came, He says: 'Come and follow Me.' Today's children are tomorrow's future.[1]

God uses kids! This is not in the sense that they are simply tools, vulnerable to being manipulated by an uncaring, omnipotent deity. Rather, children are useful to Him in His purposes for His world. Why is this? Is it partly for the same reason that Jesus took a child as a visual aid, telling His audience that unless we become as a child, we will not see the Kingdom, enter the Kingdom or be great in the Kingdom? Ever since He spoke those words, they have never ceased to be controversial, as adults have sought to defend their adult-hood, and argue the case for adult intelligence and maturity. In so doing, many have missed the point and failed to realise how children are so open to God's voice and guidance by virtue of a simple faith that has so often confounded the wise (see Matt. 11:25).

'If only my master would see the prophet who is in Samaria!

1

He would cure him of his leprosy.' These are the only recorded words of a young girl, taken captive from her own country of Israel and put into service as maid to the wife of Naaman, commander of the Syrian army. The result was a miraculous healing of this dreaded disease, and the conversion of this important person to the faith of the God of Israel (2 Kgs 5:15–18). God used this young girl – a child. We should not treat this incident lightly, for there was a bigger miracle involved. Jesus' own account of the story in Luke 4:27 says that Naaman was the first and last to be healed of such a disease in the time of Elisha, the prophet concerned. Thus the little girl made a claim for Elisha that had no precedent. Elisha had never before healed someone of a skin disease, yet the girl knew he could do it. Surely God had revealed something to that child, whether or not she was aware of it. Is it not also a marvel that this slave had compassion for her master, rather than the expected reaction of 'serves him right!' In the Bible we can also read about David the shepherd boy who fought and killed a giant in God's name; and it was a boy, Samuel, who heard God speaking when few others at that time could hear. God uses kids!

In the county of Armagh in Northern Ireland, there is an account of a boy in the last century who came under conviction of sin as he came to school. He was crying uncontrollably, and so the teacher asked another boy to take the distressed youngster home. However, on the way this other boy led him to Christ, and they immediately returned to school, full of unspeakable joy! More children apparently came under conviction and made their way into the school playground, where they knelt in tears and repentance. Parents and clergy were called in to counsel those affected, and the school was not emptied until eleven that night! Many adults were affected by this as revival spread throughout Armagh.

There are many similar historical accounts of children who

have been amongst the first, if not actually the first, to respond to the moving of the Spirit of God in sovereign power.

In more recent years the Holy Spirit fell on a group of children praying in St Andrew's school in Singapore, resulting in them speaking in tongues. This is recognised as one of the prime events that led to the Anglican Diocese of Singapore becoming a renewed Church, with almost complete acceptance and practice of charismatic gifts in church life. God uses kids!

At a parish weekend, children were led into an experience of the Holy Spirit, and many received pictures from God. One ten-year-old boy shared his picture with the adults attending the event, and the vicar stood and thanked him for that 'word from the Lord'. The boy did not know the meaning of his picture, for he described what is sometimes called a 'sleeping policeman' – a concrete hump across a road designed to slow down traffic. As a church, this congregation was being swept up by charismatic renewal. There were calls for so many changes in response, but the vicar sensed that the boy's picture was a message from God to 'slow down' and not be too hasty! God uses kids!

In 1989, a mother wrote and told me her story. She had recently received rather bad facial scarring as a result of an accident, and was to need surgery to remove it. Her children, aged five and six, said, 'We don't like your face being all scarry – we want to ask Jesus to make it better.' She said that they proceeded to lay hands on her and pray in tongues, the result of which was that she no longer needed surgery!

There are numerous stories of children praying for healing for their friends – adults included – and seeing instant results. I have seen the wonder of children realising that God is using them, as back pains, toothaches and headaches have ceased, partial sight has been restored in full and many other kinds of healing have taken place. God uses kids!

God cares for children

Children are important to God, as the Bible makes clear. In the Old Testament we read of the importance of children in ensuring the continuity of the people of God, natural enough to any ethnic group. Some commentators simply see God's intervention as helping this process, as in the case of Abraham and Sarah (Gen. 17:19) and the Hebrews in Egypt (Exod. 1–2). However, some see more in the way the Bible describes and implies God's care for children. The frequent commands to teach the Law to children, to impress it upon children (Deut. 4:9; 6:7; 11:19 etc.) may simply be seen as a means of continuing a faith as well as a race, but other passages infer that children were very much part of the congregation, e.g. Joshua 8:35. In the book of Nehemiah, those 'who are able to understand' (which included children) were among those who heard and received the Law (Neh. 8:2–8) and who committed themselves to follow that Law (Neh. 10:28,29).

We read of God's call for social justice, to care for 'the fatherless and the widows' (e.g. Deut. 14:29), and when we look at the attitude Jesus had to children, we learn even more.

A conference met with the title 'Good News to the Poor', taking the phrase from Isaiah 61, the passage Jesus claimed to be fulfilled in His ministry (Luke 4:16–21).[2] One of the first tasks it undertook was to define what was meant by 'the poor'.

After much discussion, the conference came up with the following definition:

> The poor are those who have
> no money
> no voice
> no power.

I immediately saw how children are among those who are at the heart of God's concern, for they are (with other groups) the 'poor' of the Church. Even if we consider them to have more money than we had at their age, children are not wage earners, they have no money of their own and are not among the financial supporters of the Church. Very few children have a place in church councils, in my experience. Occasionally there are a few teenagers, but in most cases, children are represented by an adult who acts as their spokesperson. As a consequence, they have little power in affecting what goes on in the local church.

Outside the Church, the situation is much the same, although much more is being said about children's rights, and the introduction of the Children Act was an important event in British history. However, the point is that God cares for children, for He sent His Son to bring 'Good News to the Poor'.

Jesus had time for children. In the incident recorded by three of the Gospel writers about little children being brought to Jesus, we cannot fail to notice that Jesus *wanted* the children to come to Himself. He was angry (indignant) that His disciples tried to protect Him from these little ones, and rebuked them strongly. Jesus was on His way to Jerusalem, and perhaps the disciples thought He was in a hurry. However, Jesus made time for the children, time enough to take them in His arms (hug them), to lay His hands on them and bless them. We do not know how many children there were, but surely this would have taken valuable time, which Jesus considered worth giving to little children (Matt. 19:13–15; Mark 10:13–16; Luke 18:15–17).

As we continue to look through the Bible to determine God's will and plan for children, we come to Peter's Pentecost sermon, and the promise of the Holy Spirit, which, he tells his audience, 'is for you and your children ... '

(Acts 2:39). Although some writers clearly used the word 'children' affectionately to mean 'children in the Lord' (e.g. in the letters of John), it is children who were expected to read or receive instructions to 'obey your parents in the Lord' (Eph. 6:1). Are they not similarly expected to receive the other commands and exhortations that are appropriate to them? Children are included in God's family. God's will and plan for His people includes children, just as they were, in all likelihood, included in the households that were baptised following the conversion of the head of those families (e.g. Acts 16:29–34).

Contemporary prophecy

Yet another element which helps us to see God's will and plan for children is in the number of contemporary prophecies which have been recorded in recent years. Contemporary prophesy can never be taken at the same value as that contained in the Bible, for, as St Paul reminds us, 'we prophesy in part' (1 Cor. 13:9) – it is imperfect. However, it is a gift of the Holy Spirit, not to be despised, and 'others should weigh carefully what is said' (1 Cor. 14:29).

Here are just some of the prophecies that have come to my notice:

> ... I will be with you, a great strength of joy, and you will pick your children up in your arms and give them to Me, and I will fill them with joy, too, and they will be able to laugh and sing and lead you sometimes in the way.
>
> Humble yourselves, My people, for your little children are waiting for the life of My Spirit to flow through them, too, that they may enter into the life of their Father which I have made for them from the foundation of the world.[3]

Jean Darnall, a well-known American lady who lived and ministered in this country for many years, received this vision in the mid 1960s:

> I saw the British Isles with many little lights all over it, and as the Lord drew me closer to it I saw they were fires that were burning from the top of Scotland to Land's End. And then I saw lightning come and contact those fires as many of them had made bright spots in different parts of the nation. There were explosions of fire and streams of fire flowed from Scotland downward over the nation, over from Ireland, down through Wales, right down to the coast, and at the Channel, some of those streams didn't stop. They flowed right across, those rivers into Europe, and spread out there.

In 1987 she went to Scotland to tell Christians there that she felt the time had come for the second part of the vision to begin to be fulfilled:

> Watch for the children that God will remarkably reveal Himself to. Children between the ages of 8, 9 to 15 will begin to see the Lord. They will have visions and dreams of the Lord ... These children will start coming, telling about healing they have received, telling about a beautiful man they have seen and wondering who He is. And the Church's task will be to help to teach these children how to love, and to teach them the Word of God.
> I feel that this is not only a word for Scotland, but I believe it's going to be a worldwide unusual awakening amongst girls and boys very soon. They will produce for the world mighty Christian leaders in the future, so watch for that, and if you are interested in children's ministry, just ask the Lord to expand your faith and give you ears to

hear and eyes to see, so that you will recognise these children – that you won't laugh down their experience or minimise what God is doing in their lives. Teach them love and teach them the Word of God.

At the Canterbury Christian Family Conference in 1987, Jean Darnall spoke about the things that would show that the second part of the vision was beginning to be fulfilled, and said:

He's going to come to them [the children] in visions and in dreams. He's going to make Himself known to boys and girls who are in non-Christian homes, in homes of violence, in homes where there is no love, in homes where there is no family continuity and care and tenderness – but Jesus is going to come to these children and they will start appearing. They'll start coming to their teachers and to other people or other Christians that they will meet, and tell about their unusual dreams and visions of the Lord. The Lord is already doing it, friends, so don't play down what these kids tell you when the Lord appears to them – when they come to you and tell you these unusual experiences. And some of these little kids won't have churchy language, you know, they don't come from Christian families, so they are not going to say it right, the way we are used to hearing it, but they will be telling about unusual experiences. When the time comes, give them the nurture and the wisdom and the love they need, because they are future leaders in the Church of the Lord Jesus Christ, and will become mightily used of the Lord.

Start expecting unusual things to happen to the children you are teaching, because the Spirit of the Lord is preparing their hearts to receive the fullness of the Holy Ghost, to receive gifts of the Holy Spirit, to receive healing, to receive ministries of healing to others as the Lord uses these children.

Another series of prophecies reported from 'schools of prophecy' held in September and October 1989 said similar things:

A word of revelation that was received and confirmed at all three conferences was that this generation of children is special to the Lord ... The present generation of children will be privileged to witness a great move of God worldwide as the Spirit of the Lord moves among the nations to strengthen His church and prepare the way for the coming of the Lord Jesus. None of us knows the exact timing of this event ... we should recognise the signs of the times to be aware of the nearness of His coming.[4]

There was a cautionary note in this report that reminds us of the responsibilities God places on us as adult believers, to be vigilant in prayer for the children: 'Because this generation of children has a special significance in God's timetable detailing the outworking of His purposes, they are inevitably the special target of the enemy. There is a great urgency for believers to reach children with the Gospel.'

The 'Toronto Blessing'

In the beginning of 1994, a Vineyard church located near Toronto Airport in Canada began to experience an unusual outpouring of the Holy Spirit. Others have written in detail of what God has been doing, and the unusual manifestations observed in many who were affected. Thousands of Christians from this country and around the world have visited that church since, and it appears that when they return home and share what God has done, in many cases the Holy Spirit comes in power and similar manifestations occur. It has been termed the 'Toronto Blessing', and has drawn much comment – and criticism.

What is not generally known is that whole families have attended that Vineyard church, including children, and many of them have received this supernatural visitation. Children are also involved in the ministry to the many visitors that fellowship receives. At the 1994 New Wine camp at the Royal Bath and West Showground, large numbers of children were similarly affected, with many slowly slumping to the ground – 'my legs went heavy' – many laughing for a long time, others crying, but most simply 'resting in the Spirit', and receiving beautiful pictures and visions of Jesus, the cross, heaven and angels. Parents were astonished when they came to collect their children, for the sight before them resembled a battlefield! They were moved and amazed, however, when opportunity came for them to receive ministry from their own children, and they found God doing through them what they had expected only to happen through the adult ministry teams in the other part of the camp. This was unusual enough to produce coverage by the national press, which tended to be alarmist in the way it was reported.

Similar stories have emerged from other events, large and small, though it must be said this was not new. What was significant, however, was the scale at which these things were reported as happening.

What has this to do with God's will and plan for children? Isn't this merely some mass hallucination or brain-washing, as some 'experts' have declared? It is true to say that children can be persuaded to 'manifest' supernatural phenomena, and this will be examined in a later chapter. My reason for raising this experience here is to suggest that this *may* be part of the 'unusual manifestations of the Lord' mentioned in those prophecies earlier. I would go as far as to say that many children's workers are convinced that this is the foretaste of what is to happen. There is an urgency in our task as we prepare children for what God is going to do through them. There is an urgency in our task to prepare the Church to receive their ministry, to respond to the prophetic word to 'give them the nurture and the wisdom and the love they need' for it is beginning to happen.

In C.S. Lewis's book, *The Lion, the Witch and the Wardrobe*, the inhabitants of Narnia saw the signs of spring after the long winter enforced by the witch, and the word went round, 'Aslan is on the move.' I see the signs of spring in this and other countries, and can only conclude, 'God is on the move' – and children are a major part of His plan!

2

Pathology – where we seem to go wrong with children

In England, less than 15 per cent of children under fifteen years of age are in a church-related activity on a typical Sunday. This was the startling fact highlighted by *All God's Children?*, the 1991 Report to the General Synod of the Church of England. The figures were drawn from the 1989 English Church Census. This alone is bad, especially when compared with earlier statistics that indicate the proportion was more like 70 per cent some thirty years earlier. However, the report went on to make this point:

It might be argued that a figure of 14 per cent is encouraging in that it is 4 per cent better than the figures for adult church attendance. That, however, would be to ignore two sobering facts. First, that past experience shows that only between 2 and 5 per cent of children attending Sunday School or children's church stayed on into adult church attendance (*Sunday Schools Today*, 1957). Second, that our present adult figures are, at least partly, the fruit of times when Sunday School attendances were considerably higher than they are today.[1]

When one considers all the man-hours put into Sunday School teaching over the years, the patient, loving care given by so many, often at great personal cost, it produces a huge sense of dismay. What can we learn from looking back? Pathology is the study of disease; 'Church Pathology' was a term used by the Church Growth movement of the 1970s in an attempt to examine some of the factors that caused a church to be unhealthy or 'diseased'. If we are to move forward in children's ministry, we must always look back, and learn from the past while identifying what God is calling us to do now.

All God's Children? made some valuable attempts to examine what had gone wrong, because it was particularly concerned with the 86 per cent who are staying outside the Church. It helpfully pointed out that the dramatic loss was not just because of the inadequacy of the teaching in the Sunday Schools of those years. It was largely also due to what the report called 'the death of a national custom' – that Sunday School was no longer part of the British way of observing Sunday. Times change, and the Church has been slow to recognise the changes in parental attitudes and the increasing range of counter-attractions. Indeed, from my personal observations, many local churches still seem to be oblivious to these social changes. It seems they cannot understand why their uninspiring offering of a Sunday School, with its inadequate resources and untrained personnel, does not attract the local youngsters!

We cannot ignore the impact of television. It was not only the Church that suffered, but so many other social, communal activities – including the cinema. It is interesting to see how cinemas have fought back, despite the 'video revolution'. They have changed, and they are not so numerous, but the multi-screen cinemas are enjoying reasonable success, it seems. Are there clues here for the Church to learn? Television has also made children come to expect high standards of presentation as the norm – it is hard for the Church to compete.

However, it is not just television that presents such

challenges. I began to realise this many years ago, as a young Church Army evangelist engaged in one of the annual summer beach missions. We spoke from a simple, wooden stand, and held up a few pictures as visual aids. But this was no match for the bright lights, the noise and colour of the fairground just a few yards away from our site. What we were 'selling' was of much more worth and importance, but the packaging was not attractive enough to those who needed it.

The improved standards of living have produced many other changes that contribute to the challenge of the task before us. Increased mobility and employment distribution have contributed to the breakdown of the nuclear family. Grandparents, aunts and uncles are likely to be living miles away, and Sundays are often designated for family visits. Sports and other recreational activities (including those laid on by the schools) are also strong competitors for available free time. Because of economic pressures, in many families both parents are in full-time employment, and Sunday is the only day in which to tackle normal household chores. The changes in Sunday trading regulations in 1994 have also produced an impact on the nature of Sunday in some places, especially where there are large shopping centres and malls. (Few churches seem to have recognised this as an opportunity, and most see it as a threat or at least a further symbol of the decline of the nation!)

These factors affect Christian children, not just the unchurched, and we must always take them into consideration. Many churches have already done so, and Sunday School is now often a midweek activity. However, this may not help the adult church, for if we are to enable parents to worship, some facility may be required for their children on Sundays. In many churches the answer is family, or all-age worship.

The shift to this kind of worship was more often a response to another realisation: 'The "School" model was an inappropriate context for learning Christ' ... Others saw the shortcomings ... Increasingly the theme that emerged was that children ought to learn about Christ in the context of the Christian community at worship.'[2]

Suggestions and further comments will be found in a later chapter about the importance of worship for children.

There are three other factors that, I believe, contribute somewhat to failures of children's ministry – poor resources, poor attitudes and poor expectations.

Poor resources

By this I mean material resources – the equipment and materials used – and human resources – those who do the work.

Material resources – places, equipment and materials. Relatively few Anglican churches, except those built in the latter half of this century, have the benefit of adequate space to do much that they would like to do. Many do not even have a church hall, or even a toilet! For them, any solution is probably very expensive, even if they could get planning permission! However, why is it the children who generally have to 'make do'? There is a principle behind the question, but I would probably be the first to acknowledge that the traditional church building is ill-suited to current practice of children's ministry (even for some adult ministry!). Those who belong to other denominations are more often blessed with better plant, though children may still often get the poorer rooms. Children, however, are much more resilient and used to second-best. At one inner-city Georgian church I visited, the children left the nicely decorated nave halfway through the service, descending into a rather damp, and not very pleasant, cellar for their classes. I was rather horrified, but when I asked the children if they would prefer to stay upstairs in the warm, they said 'no', because they preferred what they did downstairs to what the adults were doing upstairs!

Even today, there are churches that have little or no budget for their children's work, where the children's collection pays for the materials they use. There is little quality in what they have. Compared with the local school, the church seems years out of date. Clearly, the local church does not have the finance that the school may have, but with careful advice and wise spending, it could be equipped with the main necessities. (It may come back to the problem of where to store it, however!) We are investing in children, but many adults do not have a long-term view. In many churches, it is the committed teachers who provide equipment at their own expense, because they care for the children. In other churches, teachers have to make do with what they scrape together. However, as Chris Leach says, 'Children enjoy making things, but . . . They can tell quality when they see it, and they'll value it much more than something made of a yoghurt pot and a loo-roll which their teacher has so obviously fished out of her swing-bin for them.'[3]

We are living in a time when the range of teaching resources and materials has never been so great, yet still lessons are often boring, because of poor preparation of both the material and the teacher.

Human resources – the people who do the work. In too many churches, those who teach our children leave much to be desired. I appreciate their willingness and the work they put in, but many are not gifted or anointed for the task. Can we really excuse the appeal for 'any volunteers to help look after the children'? We would be horrified if this were the practice in our normal day schools, but I realise that being unpaid volunteers affects the matter.

Bishop Gavin Reid tells of his first task as bishop, on entering his office. This was to sign a large number of documents authorising lay-people to help in the administration of Holy Communion. He commented that he never had to authorise those who would teach children in the Church; 'Any heretic may do that!' he commented.

There are many organisations that offer appropriate training to those who work with children in the local church, but relatively few avail themselves of what is on offer. Many of those, like myself, who are involved in such training find themselves 'preaching to the converted', while those who should be attending training sessions are not there!

Even basic lessons need to be learnt. For instance, in most training courses it is emphasised that preparation needs to be done at least two or three days beforehand. However, all too many continue to do their preparation on the Saturday evening or even the Sunday morning!

Can clergy or service leaders get away with such inadequate preparation for adult worship? I acknowledge that there may be a few such ministers, and that emergencies often make planned preparation time impossible, but as normal practice it is totally unacceptable. Why should this not be true for children's ministry?

About music, too, I find a strange attitude that sees the need for the organist/choir/music group to meet to rehearse for adult worship, but very rarely for children's worship.

Children, as well as adults, need anointed ministers – those who have a clear gifting from God. Why is it that, in so many churches, anyone with such a clear gifting is automatically given a role within the adult church?

The Children Act 1989 has led to church authorities recommending to congregations that those who work with their children should sign a declaration that they have no criminal record regarding children. From my enquiries, many clergy have not bothered implementing this recommendation. Because of the voluntary nature of the children's work, there is no legal requirement to sign such a declaration. However, if secular society sees the need for such protective steps, why are clergy so reluctant? Sadly, there often seems to be little care over the appointment of those who work with children in the local church, on the basis that it does not really matter, as long as someone is doing it. As I know from my own observations, the result is that there are many teaching in Sunday Schools who are there because they have difficulty relating to adults, who rarely attend adult worship, or whose theology leaves much to be desired. I wish to make it clear that I am discussing pathology here – the study of disease. The scenario I am painting is made of extremes. I am foremost among those who pay homage to the thousands of teachers and leaders who are gifted, called, trained and blessed by God in their ministry, but often they are the ones who share my despair when I mention these things.

Why is it that so many churches find it hard to get the right people to work with children? There are many answers. Even where individuals are approached after much prayer for guidance, many do not want to be committed, or are scared of the 'life sentence' – afraid that once they get involved there is no way out! Many others are afraid of handling undisciplined children. Still others feel they do not know enough to teach others, although there are hundreds of Christians who would testify that they grew most in their own faith and knowledge in the process of keeping 'one step ahead' of the children they were teaching! There is a tradition in most children's groups for each small-group leader to be a teacher. However, an alternative approach is to let those who have a gift of teaching do so 'from the front'. The role of the small-group leader is then a matter of helping the children to respond and to see how the teaching applies to their particular circumstances. However, not everyone is a gifted small-group leader, and more help is needed in this matter.

Another reason many do not respond to God's call to work with children is the fear that they will miss out on what God is doing in the adult church. Many adults do not expect God to do much with children, especially, it seems, in charismatic churches! All too often, the children's ministry is given a low priority and is seen as a kind of 'holding operation' until the children become (older) teenagers, when they can become 'proper' Christians, responsible members of the church. There is often a desire to see children come into a real experience of faith, to know Jesus as their Friend, but their contribution to church life can only begin when they are 'old enough' (whatever that means).

Poor attitudes

Repeatedly I have found that the biggest obstacle to children's ministry in the local church is the attitude of adult members to the children. If many ministers are so preoccupied by the adult ministry that they are only too glad that 'someone is doing it', many more adult members of local churches display an unloving and unsympathetic attitude to children. I have observed this in many ways.

While many adult church members hope that children will come to a real faith in Christ, many more do not believe this to be real faith until the child is of an age to understand. (This kind of argument is one used by those who would deny children the bread and wine at Holy Communion.) Again, the Sunday School (or whatever it is called) is regarded as a kind of 'spiritual crèche' or child-minding facility. In one church where I was on the staff, we found it difficult to get adult church members to become 'prayer partners' with the small groups of children in the Sunday School. They did not realise the spiritual significance of this task. Part of the problem is that adults tend to measure spirituality by adult criteria. There is the tendency to think real faith leads to real maturity, and if there is little sign of maturity, there can be little faith!

The attitudes of non-Christian parents can also be a problem. Many churches (and especially Sunday Schools) do not visit people's homes very much. This can often lead to misunderstanding of motives, which can work both ways. Parents may not be too happy if the child they sent to Sunday School becomes 'religious' and starts to criticise their attitudes or habits because of what he is told at Sunday School. They may be even more alarmed if their child comes home and announces she can now speak in tongues and promptly does so! Many parents simply expect their child to have the same kind of 'religious moral teaching' they had when they were children. God used to do supernatural things, but no longer! Such things, they suppose, belong to the occult, and are not part of proper Christianity!

From the other point of view, non-Christian parents are often seen as either 'the enemy' from whose godless ways the child must be rescued, or the real targets of evangelistic attention. Indeed, as *All God's Children?* identified, the motivation for much family worship was 'less a desire to reach children in themselves and more as an evangelistic strategy to reach young parents'.[4] Many non-Christian parents see Sunday School as just another club to which their children belong. They see no problem in making a last-minute decision to take their child somewhere else on a Sunday, without any apology or even advising the Sunday School. This attitude often means last-minute changes to dramas due to be performed that day, despite weeks of preparation and rehearsal!

Perhaps, at their worst, non-Christian parents mock their

children and dissuade them from their daily Bible reading and 'quiet time', and spiritual growth is stunted or slowed down until the child gains more independence, usually in teenage years.

However, in my experience, adult problems are most acute when it comes to services in church. Different churches have different general attitudes. In one church no one seems to mind what the children do, just as long as they are happy. In another, the atmosphere is so repressive that children hate to be there. Neither, I think, is helping children to learn what worship is about, and how to learn to love worship and grow in it.

Many adults simply want the children to be kept away so that they do not 'spoil' the worship. It matters little what the children do, as long as they are happy, they come, and they do not disturb the adults at worship. One cannot blame many parents who have this attitude, especially mothers whose partner does not share their faith (it is seldom the other way round). Many such parents have little freedom to attend church services, and are desperate to enjoy fellowship and communion with God. My wife, Carol, often said of family services that 'it's all right for you up front leading the service. I'm the one who has to have eyes everywhere, making sure the children aren't causing chaos for others!'

If children are to come into church, they are expected to be everything God has not made them – keeping quiet, enjoying long hymns and prayers, maintaining long periods of concentration, and occupying, without fidgeting, very uncomfortable seats called 'pews'! Often no one explains the 'ground rules' to new parents, or even to children themselves. This may mean that many adults are annoyed or disgusted when children run round, climb into the pulpit, pile up kneelers or do the many other things children do when they get bored. In many churches adults clearly expect children to be illiterate and/or destructive; I have been where children are not given notice sheets or orders of service, but are given the hymn books with missing pages and covers. This is the welcome they receive!

Young choristers are sometimes cited as examples of good church behaviour, looking so angelic, enjoying 'proper' church music and being good, but as one who often sits near them waiting for my opportunity to preach, I tend to feel sorry for them. They seem to enjoy their singing, and dutifully take part in the liturgy. However, during the prayers and the sermon they are often bored, and I see them playing cards or pencil and paper games, or even reading. (I have occasionally seen adult choristers do the latter! They think they cannot be seen because they are up in the chancel!)

What of those churches where adults are so pleased to have children there that they put up with anything to keep the children happy? Children may feel in some ways 'at home', but what are they learning about God and the worship of His people? Are they not in danger of learning that this consecrated (set aside) building is just another playground, but with fewer toys? Is God present, or not? How is that communicated to children? Children need to learn about the awesomeness of God, but only if the adults genuinely experience it. In some churches, little children soon learn that you only have to yell and you are taken out to a nice room where there are toys to play with! Is this the right lesson to learn?

Poor expectations

This is the third area that I feel contributes to the failure of much children's ministry. I see it in different ways. For instance, when I invited the local head teacher to address the Sunday School staff of a church, one comparison I saw was in the area of expectations. Children in the school were often given responsibility. I saw that this was easier in a school where children *had* to attend, and were not at the whim of unthinking parents, or a rival attraction.

But in general, we do not expect much of the children in the Church. I have sometimes made a sweeping generalisation that much of children's ministry worldwide is confined to 'teaching children the Bible, and telling them to be good'. Not that there is anything wrong with this, but it is so restricted.

Children in the Way, the 1988 Report that preceded *All God's Children?*, dared to suggest that rather than being 'in the way' of real Christianity, children are 'people with needs to be met and a contribution to make to the life of the Church . . . [they] must be acknowledged as those who sometimes lead the way'.[5] But few churches get beyond what I call the 'R' factor. I mean the reaction of most adult Christians when children participate in church worship, by reading a lesson, singing a song, leading prayers, etc. When this happens, adults often give a patronising smile and say, 'Aahh!' Culturally, we do not expect much of children. Because of our maturity and wisdom, we, as adults, give to children. That is the way of things. We accept the sentimental stories of things children have said and done which have melted adult hearts, but this is not the norm. Our only hope is that children grow up nicely, to be like us, perhaps to fulfil our unfulfilled aims, but it is all in the future, when they are 'old enough'. Our expectations are limited by our own experience and we seldom think about what is happening to our children.

When adults see or hear of children being used powerfully by God, they are amazed, especially when they are informed that this can be quite normal! At the summer New Wine camp, I seek to train the leaders of small groups to be primarily leaders and facilitators, enabling the children with experience and Bible knowledge to share it with those who may have neither one nor the other. The children may not do it as well as we might, and are often reluctant at first. However, when they see that we are taking them seriously, and that this is something that God wants them to do, they generally respond. So many of our children know Bible facts, but need help in shaping their lives and attitudes, and in ministering it to others. (This is also true of very many adult church members.)

The South American pastor, Juan Carlos Ortiz, in his book, *Disciple*, told how he would generally preach on a subject for as much as six months, and would only change the subject when he saw the congregation beginning to act on what he was teaching.

How brave he was! Much current teaching material for use in Sunday Schools and other children's groups has a set lesson for each week. I feel that one problem of such dated teaching material is that we become 'task oriented', and that teaching becomes a matter of 'completing the lesson'. Whether the children have actually learnt the lesson seems to be immaterial, for the syllabus dictates that we move on to the next lesson next week. One of the things often missing from Christian education is what might be called feedback. In day school, children have various tests, to assess not only knowledge, but also understanding. Children are given various incentives to encourage their growth, to let them know they have achieved certain goals. For most children, this in itself is an incentive to do even better. What most children's groups fail to do is to help children to see what they are achieving.

It is easy to test knowledge of Bible facts, but it is more difficult to measure understanding. This can be done best in small group discussion, problem setting, or even writing a song or a sketch. When you feel a child understands a fact rather than simply being able to recite it, the child should be praised and encouraged.

Someone told me many years ago, 'the purpose of teaching

is that others learn!' If they are not learning, we are not teaching! Even so, it may be an unreal expectation that our children's workers should be as competent as those who have had the benefit of three years of full-time training!

For me, however, as well as the weakness of much of our biblical teaching, the other area of failure is not to recognise that children learn far more by what they do. Children learn most by copying. The problem is that adult Christians often give them little to copy, or at least we give them a different version! For instance, how many of us teach children to put their hands together and close their eyes to pray? Yet how many of us assume that posture when we pray? It is said that faith is caught, rather than taught. How do we do this? I have been in situations where Sunday School teachers do not want me to teach children to pray for healing because they do not want the children to be disappointed! What kind of faith is that? In my experience, the resilience of children means that they are well able to cope with some of the mystery involved in topics such as healing and prayer in general. As the American pastor/teacher, John Wimber, says, 'Faith is spelt R.I.S.K.!' There is always the element of risk when one steps out in faith, yet we can learn how to take small steps at first, gaining increasing confidence as we see God answer our prayers.

I have been a Church Army evangelist for more than twenty years. One lesson I have learnt in that period is that we are best equipped to reach our peers for Christ. Young married couples are best equipped to reach other young married couples, men to reach other men, the elderly to reach the elderly, teenagers to reach teenagers, etc. If we expect evangelism only to be done by the professional evangelist, then the task has no hope of succeeding. With all my heart I believe that the most effective force to be mobilised to reach the 86 per cent of unchurched children in England today is the 14 per cent in our churches. Anglican children are baptised and commissioned with the prayer that they 'continue Christ's faithful soldier and servant' to the end of their life. Service is part of normal Christianity, and evangelism is part of the natural breathing rhythm of the Church. We should work for, and expect, children not only to learn the truths of the Gospel, but to grow in the Spirit. We should expect to see them manifesting the 'fruit of the Spirit' – love, joy, peace, patience, kindness, goodness, faithfulness, gentleness and self-control – and learning to do the works of the Gospel – evangelism, healing, and good works 'which God prepared in advance for us to do' (Eph. 2:10).

We need to learn to balance our learning programme, balancing cerebral or cognitive learning with affective or experiential learning, teaching children, we may say, to know the words of Jesus and do the works of Jesus. It is this learning that is the subject of this book.

3

Where are we heading?

The ship had been sailing for months across the open seas. The Captain was good at his job and kept a tight, happy ship. Everyone was content. The crew got on with their various tasks efficiently, and the passengers enjoyed their care and the pleasures of the voyage.

A welcome sight was another ship travelling in the same waters. From one such vessel a small boat was launched and a visitor received.

'Where are you heading for?' the visitor enquired.

'We're going this way,' the Captain replied.

'But where are you heading – what is your destination?' said the visitor, a little puzzled.

'Well, we're just heading in this sort of direction,' the Captain said. 'As long as the passengers are happy, and we're doing our job, everything will be fine! If we had a definite destination, we might not get there, or we might go the wrong way. Then people would be disappointed, so we just keep everything running nicely, just sailing in this direction!'

A ridiculous story, but in some ways it illustrates the way in which much children's ministry is exercised. It doesn't seem to matter what is done, as long as it is done and everyone is happy! When asked to write down the three main aims of the children's work in their church, many children's workers are generally flummoxed. After a moment or two they start writing, but it is clear that this is a new idea to most of them. It would seem that no one has really sat down to consider where the children's work is heading, and what it should seek to achieve. There is an assumption that everyone knows what it is about, and everyone should just get on and do it, rather like the ship's Captain in the story above.

One of the more exciting recent trends has been in the area of setting aims and objectives in children's ministry. It cannot be denied that many children are lost to Christ and His Church through boredom. Some of the reasons for this have already been spelt out in an earlier chapter. Consider the effect of a children's ministry that has had careful and prayerful thought in deciding where it is going, how long it is going to take to get there, and what it is going to take to achieve it. Consider the effect on the team of workers, as well as the children, because they feel the active support of the rest of the congregation who see their work as a vital ingredient in the well-being of the church. Consider the possibilities of a church that is seeking to respond to the movement of the Holy Spirit, and eagerly desiring the children to be included in what God is doing. This is a reality in a growing number of churches, and it could be in yours! However, any aims in children's ministry must be set in the context of the aims for the rest of the membership of the local church.

Mission statement

It is currently fashionable for charities and organisations to have a 'mission statement'. This is a memorable sentence or two that summarises what the organisation is for, and what it aims to do. Many churches have adopted the practice, and some have followed it up by establishing aims within the different membership groups within the church, all of which support that overall mission statement. One such statement that has been adapted by many churches is: 'To know Christ better, and make Him better known'.

Many will think this is an unnecessary exercise. The Church is here to preach the Gospel – isn't that enough of a mission statement? But churches differ in character, dependent, possibly, on the history of each one. For instance, a church built as part of the Oxford Movement, the Anglo-Catholic revival in the late 1830s, will often maintain that spirituality. Part of its mission statement (even if unwritten) will probably be a commitment to the Anglo-Catholic approach to biblical interpretation and liturgical practice. By contrast, a fellowship established as a product of the early years of the charismatic movement may shun any kind of liturgical structures, and perhaps place an emphasis on shared leadership, or on the place of contemporary prophecy in church life. This is because at that time so many felt able to express their new-found spiritual freedom only outside the denominational structures. This latter church may write elements of this emphasis into its mission statement, because it feels strongly that this is what God is calling the church to do.

There are other influences that help form the character of a church. A particularly popular or gifted minister can often be the determining factor, and so a church becomes known for its effective evangelism, or teaching, or social action, or its young people's work, etc. The point is that the children's ministry is only part of the local church, and that the connection needs to be borne in mind, otherwise a parallel church is formed, which actually bears little or no resemblance to the parent body. This may, of course, be deliberate!

What is the history of your church fellowship? Does it have any effect on its 'present character'?

What is, or what do you think would be, the mission statement of your church?

Values

The degree to which children's ministry features in the aims of a local church is often affected by the values placed on children. Values are an important ingredient, for they are the foundation stones on which we base the things we do and the reasons we do them. They are the basic guidelines and understanding on which aims and goals are built. They say something about our attitudes to children, our biblical and sociological understanding, and the worth and value we place on them as part of the family of the church.

The biblical understanding of children has been partly examined in chapter 1. It will become obvious that I am convinced of the scriptural interpretation that sees children as having a relationship with God, based on the words of Jesus, 'the Kingdom of God belongs to such as these' (Mark 10:14, etc.). Some may wish to change this value statement, perhaps saying, 'Children may enter into a relationship with God.' This will be discussed in more depth in chapter 7.

Chris Leach has written of the values established for the children's ministry at St James' Church, Styvechale, Coventry, based round four 'R's:

RELATIONSHIP
Children have a relationship with God.
They have an enemy who is trying to spoil it.

RESOURCING
Children need to grow intellectually – knowing about God.
Children need to grow experientially – knowing God.
RELEVANCE
Children's ministry should invest for the future.
Children's ministry should have application now.
REALLY GOOD!
Children's ministry should be fun.
Children's ministry should have quality.[1]

I would add to these, though it makes the task of remembering them a little harder! My suggested additions would be:

RESPECT
Children are individuals worthy of respect and dignity. Their vulnerability is no excuse for demeaning or abusing them, or using them to meet my needs (Matt. 18:2–5).
RECEIVING
Children are included in the Community of Faith and may receive all that adults receive from God (Acts 2:39).
RESPONSIBILITY
Parents have the prime responsibility for the faith and nurture of their children (Eph. 6:4). The children's ministry must seek to support them whenever possible.
READY NOW
Children are useful to God now, not just when they become adults (Acts 2:17).
God reveals things to children (Matt. 11:25). Children can display a wisdom beyond their years (Job 32:7–9).

One further important value may come under another 'R':

RECREATION
Childhood is special, and I will not rob children of their childhood. By this I mean I will not apply undue pressure

to conform to adult criteria, whilst encouraging their growth into maturity (Luke 2:52).

Part of the vision of the restored Jerusalem is that of children playing (Zech. 8:5).

These are the things we believe about children. They affect our attitudes to them, and help determine our aims as regards ministry to and with them. A common problem experienced by many churches is that adults do not really think about children. They are a marginalised group, as considered in an earlier chapter. Some years ago, the United Reformed Church published a discussion document entitled *Towards a Charter for Children in the Church*. In explaining their action, they wrote at the head of their suggestions for action:

> On October 31st 1517, Martin Luther wrote out a list of 95 points or 'theses' about the way in which he thought the church should be. Having written his list, he nailed it to the church door in Wittenberg, in Germany. This simple act proved to be one of the events which triggered the Protestant Reformation.
>
> This Children's Charter may not be quite so far reaching, but we hope that it makes your church think in the way that Luther's 95 Theses did.[2]

The ten points the paper proposed are as follows:

TOWARDS A CHARTER FOR CHILDREN IN THE CHURCH

1

Children are equal partners with adults in the life of the church.

2

The full diet of Christian worship is for children as well as adults.

3

Learning is for the whole church, adults
and children.

4

Fellowship is for all – each belonging meaningfully
to the rest.

5

Service is for children to give, as well as adults.

6

The call to evangelism comes to all God's people
of whatever age.

7

The Holy Spirit speaks powerfully through children as
well as adults.

8

The discovery and development of gifts in children and
adults is a key function of the church.

9

As a church community we must learn to do only those
things in separate age groups which we cannot in all
conscience do together.

10

The concept of 'Priesthood of all believers'
includes children.[3]

Whilst this is not actually a set of aims, it is a series of value
statements which would enable a church to develop its aims
in ministry to adults and children alike. I have been pleased
to commend it to others as a useful tool in tackling the

primary hurdle to the renewal of children's ministry – the rest of the adult church!

Before continuing to read this chapter, take a moment now to write down three main aims of the children's ministry in your church.

Is this the first time you have written these aims? Are these aims already published in some kind of policy document? When were they last reviewed? Are these aims related in any way to the adult or other youth ministry of the church?

Questions like this can be uncomfortable, even threatening, but they can help us to concentrate on the God-given task before us. But what is that task? What is it that we are seeking to do with children in the Church? 'To teach them the Faith' and 'To lead them into a living relationship with God' are good aims, but are they still too vague and narrow? The whole idea of teaching, as we have seen in an earlier chapter, is that children learn, but we realise that children learn different things by different means. Educationalists also help us to understand that different children learn best in different ways: some are doers, and learn most by active participation, and some are thinkers, who learn by reading and reflecting. Some need intense leadership, others do better left to their own research and investigation. To teach children the Faith is more than imparting biblical facts, as important as that is.

Jesus commanded us to 'make disciples' (Matt. 28:19), not Bible students, or even just converts. A study of His discipleship 'methods' can bring startling conclusions, and force us to re-examine what we are doing in the Church, with adults as well as children and young people. For instance, there were clearly different groups that Jesus taught, each of which had slightly different treatment. The twelve disciples lived with Jesus for His earthly ministry, and shared everything with Him. They were the ones first commissioned 'to preach the kingdom of God and to heal the sick' (Luke 9:2). The second group may be considered to be the seventy-two others (Luke 10:1–9), who did not spend the same kind of time with Jesus as the twelve, but were sufficiently discipled to be sent out with a similar commission. Jesus also taught other groups, large and small, as well as dealing with individual questioners. One conclusion may be that Jesus taught them to *do* something, not just *know* something and *be* something. In so much of children's ministry, the only 'doing' is colouring in pictures or doing word-searches of various kinds.

But what kind of things can children do as part of their learning of the Faith? This is more easily understood and answered when one considers a more holistic concept of Christian nurture. The Christian faith affects every part of life. We are who we are in Christ in relationship to others, in the Church and beyond it.

Aims for children's ministry

The London-based Ichthus Christian Fellowship published one of the best set of aims I have seen for their children's ministry, in which it was stated that their desire was 'to teach, experience and spread the Kingdom, going for as much of the contemporary presence of heaven as possible'.[4]

The publication was a simple duplicated set of notes given to all parents and children's workers, and set out their aims as follows:

In our relationships, work and ministry to children, we are seeking to help them to be:

1. KINGDOM CHILDREN
    with a growing awareness and experience of living in
    the Holy Spirit.
2. KNOWING THE KING
    getting to know Jesus for themselves, not just involved
    in kingdom activities.
3. HAVING KINGDOM UNDERSTANDING
    learning to understand and apply God's word.
4. BEING PART OF KINGDOM COMMUNITY
    fully involved in the family life of the church.
5. INVOLVED IN KINGDOM WORK
    learning to minister to others that which they are receiv-
    ing from God. [5]

It is the holistic nature of these aims that is so attractive and
challenging. They reflect a set of values that acknowledges
the worth and dignity of children now, and sees discipleship
as more than 'knowing Bible facts and being good'.

Aims such as these reveal a particular emphasis of that
group of churches, that of having the concept of the Kingdom
of God at the heart of what they are and do. This is a
thoroughly biblical concept, for one cannot avoid the fact that
Jesus' commission was to 'preach the kingdom of God'. As
other commentators point out, the Kingdom is not so much a
geographical realm as the rule or reign of God as King of the
human heart. Thus Jesus says, 'the kingdom of God is within
you' (Luke 17:21). The snag, of course, is that today children
have no real understanding of kingship, but in practice, there
seems to be no real problem in coming to such an
understanding.

This example of aims is also strong in its element of active
participation. The last two aims, for instance, are not aca-
demic, for they require action, and the action cannot be
limited to Sundays, or when the children's groups meet. The

Ichthus Christian Fellowship address the areas of personal experience and life in the Holy Spirit, of relationship with God in Christ, of understanding the Bible, of congregation life, and of ministry. Many adults would find aims in these areas stimulating and stretching, let alone children!

Are there other areas of child-related life about which you would consider setting aims?

Try and write a set of aims that reflects the character of your church fellowship, but which addresses wider areas of the lives of children. After your initial thoughts (and discussions), commit yourself to taking time to give the matter much prayer, asking the Holy Spirit to give supernatural wisdom as well as your common sense!

Test your suggestions out with others in your church, including your minister, perhaps as a first step in establishing clear aims for your ministry to children – or as a step in revising your previously stated aims. If they are not acceptable to the leadership, work on them until they are acceptable, even if the process takes time.

Problems

By this time, you may be thinking that such ideas are impossible in your situation. This is especially true when you have the children for only twenty to thirty minutes once a week (or even less in some cases). How can you develop a programme that takes these different areas into consideration, when you need all your time to get through your teaching material? I dare to suggest that if more churches set out to teach less, more would be learnt! This takes into consideration the fact that the learning of biblical facts is only one part of Christian discipleship – an important, essential part, but still only a part. Much else is learnt in the context of relationships and doing things together.

More attention will be given to the task of nurture and growth in faith in later chapters, but it is important to consider now some of the implications of this more holistic approach. If there is only a limited amount of time available, you may conclude that although a wide approach is desirable, it is not (yet) practical. This may be reflected in planning the steps required to achieve your aims. Be aware, however, of the problem of comparison. This affects adult ministry and youth ministry, as well as children's ministry Just as no two people are identical, no two churches are the same. This means that although we may get clues and ideas from other churches, they will not necessarily work in our situation. This is because the people are different, with different backgrounds and experiences; because the leaders are different, with different skills and experience, and because of many other factors. Even if there are many similarities, there may be different time-scales. What is achievable in six months for one church may take six years in another! In some cases, the planning may need to take a five-, ten- or fifteen-year timespan. Experience would suggest that churches with thriving ministries have frequently sunk into oblivion because their planning did not look far enough ahead. Many churches are doomed to die, because elderly congregations can be near-sighted, and concerned only for the present and not the future. Long-term goals are a missing element in much thinking and planning.

Setting goals

Having such values and stated aims is an important foundation for a serious examination of our task in children's
ministry. However, there is more. At the moment, it is rather
like a game of football, in which we have acknowledged that
it is a good, wholesome game, which involves a lot of players
and has some spectator value. Each team is trying to kick the
ball in opposite directions, but there is no means by which we
can know which team has won! Knowing the direction to play
is one thing, but we need clearly defined goals by which we
can know if a team has scored.

This idea is not new to those familiar with the principles
of church growth. It was, and still is, a subject that arouses
deep suspicion, for it seems to be rather unspiritual. We
are dealing with the sovereign Almighty God, it is reasoned,
and so we cannot set objectives for God to achieve. The point
is, however, that they are our goals, determined by much
prayer and careful thought. Because they are prayerfully
determined, one may hope that they are in agreement with
Scripture and in line with the revealed will of God. That
they need God's supernatural action is no restrictive factor.
We are simply planning the steps required to achieve the
aims which we also determined by prayerful and careful
discussion.

The Bible Society puts this clearly:

Planning is an art for getting things done. The Christian
engages in planning because he knows that he is called
to act responsibly and effectively as a co-worker with
God. 'For we are partners working together for God, and
you are God's field. You are also God's building' 1 Corinthians 3:9.

On the one hand the Christian recognizes that he is

utterly dependent upon God for the achieving of spiritual results, and on the other hand he knows that he is expected to use his mind to work according to God's standards and in ways which are most likely to be effective.[6]

The writer goes on to make the important point that planning is an act of faith. It is by faith that clearly defined goals may be achieved, for 'faith is being sure of what we hope for and certain of what we cannot see' (Heb. 11:1). Goals are the steps we set out to help us see that we are achieving our aims. In a game of football the goal is marked by three white-painted pieces of wood made into a rectangular arch. The ground, too, is marked, so that there can be no doubt if team scores – the ball crosses those white lines. For the purposes of planning, there are helpful things to bear in mind in setting goals.

Good goals are relevant and they are significant. They serve our main purpose. We do not set a goal just because it seems to be a good idea. It is very easy to get diverted. For instance, if someone with particular skills comes on the scene, it often happens that new activities are planned to make use of that expertise. No one stops to think whether those new activities are significant and actually serve the aim, because we just want to use those gifts, etc.

Good goals are measurable. In some way there is a element that helps us to know whether or not we have achieved them. It may be a time reference; e.g. 'By Easter next year we will . . .' It may be numerical; e.g. 'We will increase to 120 children in each section . . .' It is this element of goal-setting that causes some Christians most difficulty, for it seems to be trying to force God to work to our deadlines. Despite the anguish, it can serve to stretch the faith of those involved. I presented this aspect of planning to the support group of a youth mission some years ago. In prayer we decided numerical targets each night for those who would make a response to the message in the Christian coffee bar we had established for the event. Everyone felt a sense of risk, for we were opening ourselves up to failure. But those young people were prayed into the Kingdom of heaven, and each night those targets were achieved or exceeded, and there was great rejoicing.

Good goals are achievable. It is useless having goals that are really beyond our hope and faith. In the youth mission mentioned above, it would have been disastrous to set a goal such as 'Every young person attending will respond to Christ . . .' If the goals are that kind of fanciful thinking, then those concerned will become discouraged, or will make excuses and deny the goal. As admirable as that intention might be, it was clearly improbable. I have been engaged in parish evangelistic missions, in which evangelism and outreach amongst the unchurched has been the goal. When it is realised that there have been no new converts, no one admits failure; rather, everyone is comforted by the statement 'But the church was blessed and built up.' This may be true, but important questions need to be asked about the original aims and objectives. It is much easier to set goals within our faith limits.

Good goals are acceptable. By this I mean that all those involved in the venture accept that it is a good goal, and agree to work with it. In children's ministry, it is not enough that the leadership sets the goals and commits the group to them. Even if the goals are divinely inspired, the other leaders and the children themselves need to agree to take them on board. This is particularly true where a goal will demand more in time, money and/or commitment.

Take a few moments to consider one of the aims – either one you have written or one from the stated examples. Applying it to your church situation, what steps would have to be taken to achieve such an aim? For example, you may need to:

Consult the children's work team and the church leadership within the next two months.

Plan a campaign of education and communication of the vision to the rest of the adult congregation, to be implemented within four months.

Planning steps

This process of planning may be rather daunting, and may feel as if it is quenching the Holy Spirit. I see no contradiction between responding to the spontaneous move of God and at the same time planning how to integrate the new discoveries into the life of the church. Such a thoughtful process will help to keep feet on the ground, and prevent people being swayed by one fashionable movement after another. It helps to keep the balance between subjective experience and objective reality. There are many in business who are able to use their expertise in the planning exercise. If this is not really possible, the following ten steps may help in the process of achieving aims. They were written in the context of church growth, but I feel they are applicable to most situations:

1. *Assess where you are at and where you have come from.* Many plans fail because they do not start at this point. We can only move ahead from the point where we have now arrived.

2. *Define goals.* The leader should do this as a preliminary step. The blind cannot lead the blind. But he should also encourage discussion of his goals and allow for amendments and additions.

3. *Establish priorities.* List the agreed goals in order of priority and give a time for the achievement of each. One cannot tackle everything at once.

4. *Marshal resources.* Estimate what will be needed for the achieving of each goal in terms of manpower and money. What resources do you estimate are already available, and what will you have to continue to pray and work for?

5. *Identify obstacles.* As far as possible, these should be indentified and anticipated before the plans are implemented. Personal explanations at an initial stage may help to lessen the tension which could otherwise build up. God may have something to say through the opposition encountered which will lead to better plans, and not simply to compromise amendments.

6. *Draw up plans.* These should specify what is to be done by when.

7. *Allocate responsibilities.* This will show who is to do what and by what date.

8. *Check progress.* At pre-selected stages the plans should contain check-points to monitor progress.

9. *Evaluate results.* Are the plans working to achieve the desired results? If not, scrap them. There is nothing sacred about the plans.

10. Reformulate plans on the basis of your experience so far, and develop them as your vision for the work further unfolds.[7]

Be excited about the vision God is giving you. Do not be discouraged, do not rush headlong into things. When God moves in revival power you and your church may be swept along to the degree that planning falls a little by the wayside, but planning will help in the days, weeks, months and years afterwards. Rwanda and Indonesia are two countries with a history of extraordinary Christian revival, yet both countries have suffered in recent months, and the lack of long-term planning seems to be evident.

4

Children and the power of the Holy Spirit – is it right?

In 1965 on the island of Timor in Indonesia, the Holy Spirit came in power. Christians felt compelled to pray, evangelistic motivation and anointing came on groups of lay-people who formed themselves into teams, 'travelling throughout Timor and the surrounding islands proclaiming the Gospel, healing the sick and raising the dead'.[1] The teams included groups of eight to ten children of primary-school age, who were anointed for intercession, and who were encouraged by prophecies or other words of wisdom or knowledge. These children's teams had equal success, it seems, in bringing adults and children to Christ, and healing the sick.

But is this the exception, rather than the rule? Despite the illustrations given earlier, many Christians are unsure about children experiencing and working in the supernatural power of God. God has moved children's evangelists to minister this teaching as part of the whole Gospel for adults and children alike for many years, but it still seems as though we are sailing in uncharted waters. 'The theology is still being written,' someone said.

This is not the place for the justification of the exercise of spiritual gifts, or for the terminology of the experience of the

Holy Spirit. However, it is important to address some of the key issues which give cause for apprehension.

The Spirit in children

The 'full' Gospel includes the fact that when someone becomes a Christian, he/she receives the Holy Spirit: '... if anyone does not have the Spirit of Christ, he does not belong to Christ' (Rom. 8:9b) – including children! On the day of Pentecost, the apostle Peter said to the crowd, 'The promise [of the Spirit] is for you and for your children ...' (Acts 2:39). 'You are all sons of God through faith in Christ Jesus, for all of you who were baptised into Christ have clothed yourselves with Christ. There is neither Jew nor Greek, slave nor free, male nor female, for you are all one in Christ Jesus' (Gal. 3:26–8). It is a fair assumption that we might also say there is neither young nor old in the question of receiving all that God has for His children. As David Walters has put it, '... children do not have a baby or junior version of the Holy Spirit'.[2]

It is natural for those who have themselves experienced the grace and power of the Spirit to seek for children to share the fullness of life in Christ. Yet many find it difficult to lead children into an actual experience of God's power, beyond, of course, that of making a step towards Jesus – the greatest experience in many ways.

In addition, although many accept the theory of children being filled with the Holy Spirit, many more are cautious about the practice.

Francis Bridger, for instance, warns of the dangers of children thinking of supernatural gifts as a version of magic – understandable in the light of the number of children's cartoons, etc. that have magical powers involved. He is also concerned about the emotional vulnerability of children and the consequences of supernatural phenomena. From a developmental point of view, he argues that as children do not have the necessary mental capabilities until adulthood, they are not able to control the use of spiritual gifts, or relate a gift to the truth about Christ. Finally, he is also concerned that the adult leader (you and me) will (unconsciously) encourage a human (counterfeit?) manifestation of a spiritual gift in a child, because the child wants to please us. [3]

Such cautions are understandable, and we must take real care not to be guilty of realising these fears. However, growing experience is proving to me that God is in all this, and that as long as we are keeping close to Him, and evaluating the criticism of others in the light of what we believe God is doing, then we probably won't go far wrong.

We must not be naïve, however. The enemy is a subtle strategist who loves to cause division and destruction. For this reason alone, we must exercise caution, and seek the supreme motivation of love. There is no room for spiritual cowboys or discontents who see children as a means of meeting their own desires and needs.

A key issue for many people concerns the 'rightness' of children receiving the experience of God's power, together with the subsequent use of various gifts of the Spirit. Is it inappropriate and, as one Sunday School teacher expressed it, '. . . like teaching a five-year-old A-level maths'?

Is it biblical?

Is the experience of spiritual gifts in children biblical? One might argue that the young slave girl who was responsible for her Syrian master finding healing of his dreaded skin disease, as discussed in chapter 1, was manifesting the spiritual gift of knowledge (2 Kgs 5:3). However, I see no specific injunction of Scripture that children specifically should or should not practise spiritual gifts. The apostle Peter said, 'The

promise [of the Spirit] is for you and for your children ... '
Scripture talks of being 'trained in righteousness', which may
or may not include the use of spiritual charismata (gifts or
manifestations of the Spirit). We cannot argue from silence,
and so we can only make a general assumption that as the
early Church grew, and as children came to faith, they were
apprenticed in the things of God. It would appear that
children were expected to hear or read the command to 'obey
your parents in the Lord, for this is right' (Eph. 6:1). I would
conclude that they were also expected to hear or read the
other scriptural commands to the Church in general, e.g. 'Be
filled with the Spirit' (Eph. 5:18)!

From a historical point of view, I have already mentioned
several examples of accounts of revivals, in which God has
used children and young people to usher in the power of the
Holy Spirit in repentance and 'signs following'. Often this
was misunderstood, but God persisted through the openness
of these young people to bless whole communities and
beyond. It is interesting to note that in most cases, after the
initial reception of the touch of divine power, children were
not encouraged to grow in this experience. For instance, when
I visited Singapore in 1994, it was clear that this next generation of children had been largely overlooked in the encouragement to live by the Spirit and to grow in the use of
spiritual gifts. They were just like so many other children in
churches round the world, receiving good Bible education,
but no expectation of active membership and discipleship
until they were older.

Is it healthy?

Is the experience of the Holy Spirit healthy, bearing in mind
the emotional vulnerability of children? A Baptist pastor
wrote a very concerned letter, saying that 'it is not only

impossible, but exceedingly dangerous to attempt ...
[because] ... there are issues that adults understand, but
which children cannot. There are experiences that adults can
bear the weight of, but that children cannot. To load the
child's mind and heart with things too heavy for it to bear is
to expose children to unnecessary pressure which may have
disastrous results ... ' I am no doctor, and although I have
received basic training in some aspects of psychotherapy,
I have no qualifications to make authoritative statements
on the matter. However, personal experience and biblical
knowledge make me conclude that I do not believe God
would give His gifts to children if they were harmful. Of
course the gifts can be abused and misused like many others
He has given. Children can seriously injure themselves and
others with a bicycle, but with training and teaching, bicycles
are a great joy and of great use. So it is with gifts of the Holy
Spirit.

One might then consider whether 'spiritual manifestations'
are 'fleshly' – i.e. counterfeit, mere actions done to please the
hero-leader, or at worst, emotional manifestations whipped
up by an unscrupulous (or misled) children's evangelist.
Penny Frank is quite honest when she says, 'The reason we
find ourselves wary of the Holy Spirit is often a commendable
one – we want to make sure that this is God and not our
imaginations at work ... It is so easy for anyone with
communication skills and training to provoke and manipulate
children to exhibit spiritual manifestations, especially in a
large group.'[4] Whereas there is much evidence of this happening in adults, I am not aware of its occurrence with children.

Is it right?

Renewal (if that is the correct term applied to children) in the
Holy Spirit is part of the 'package deal' of faith in Jesus Christ.

I strongly believe, along with many others, that the gift and experience of the Holy Spirit is 'right' for children, not least for the following reasons.

Spiritual warfare. There is an urgency which forbids us to bury our heads in the sand. The writers of the report *All God's Children?* reminded us of the very real principalities and powers that are waging war on our children, by helping us to see the commercial forces and peer pressures that have severe impact on them. Referring to the reluctance to evangelise children in case of getting it wrong, the report warns that if we do not do so, there are many others who have no such qualms.

David Walters, an Englishman who now has a ministry in the United States, shares some words from a prophecy received by himself and his wife: 'Satan is preparing his army, but My Church is entertaining her children.'[5]

There seems to be a lot of truth in that: while Satan takes the task seriously, the Christian Church treats her children as if they are immune to such dangers until they are older. There is much evidence of the activity of Satan in children – he is no respecter of their age and status. In the media reporting of the many wars that rage across our planet, we see that children are among the first victims, so why should it surprise us that this might be the case in spiritual warfare? While children have angels to watch over them (Matt. 18:10) it is ironic that the enemy uses evil spirits – fallen angels – to assault and pressurise them.

In the region of Tyre, a woman whose little daughter was possessed by an evil spirit came and fell at Jesus' feet, begging Him to drive out the demon. After some conversation in which the woman argued her case, Jesus dismissed her, saying that the demon had left her child (cf. Mark 7:24–30). Examination of the Greek text reveals that the girl was very young, and that it was an 'unclean' spirit or demon that was affecting her. One commentator concludes that the girl's demon was an impure, dirty spirit. Others may seek to determine how the child became demonised, but the point I would make is that here is an instance of a small child desperately needing to be set free from this evil spirit.

One may also look at a second incident, recorded by all three synoptic Gospel writers (Matt. 17:14–20; Mark 9:14–29; Luke 9:37–42). This time it is a boy, affected from infancy with symptoms of epilepsy, due, it is claimed, to a spirit. Some might claim that the diagnosis was wrong, and that it was inaccurate to ascribe the condition to a spirit. However, it was the Son of God who 'rebuked the evil spirit' and commanded it to come out of the child and never enter again (Mark 9:25).

It would be easy to cite modern-day examples, but I feel this may be sufficient to make my point. If we do not bring the power of the Holy Spirit to bear in the lives of our children, we may be leaving them vulnerable to the work of the enemy. Our role is to protect our children by prayer, and by teaching and training to enable them to resist 'enemy invasion', by putting on 'the armour that God provides' (a corporate, as well as an individual responsibility), by taking 'the sword of the Spirit, which is the word of God' (Eph. 6:10–17), and by 'living in the Spirit' (Gal. 5:25).

The Church of England commissions its newly-baptised to fight against 'the world, the flesh and the devil'. I for one have no doubt that they, like the rest of the Body of Christ, need the empowering of the Holy Spirit to equip them for the battle.

I believe that we arm our kids for light skirmishes with the enemy, while Satan uses his heavy artillery on them! This is due, in the main, to the fact that we do not readily have a world view that takes seriously the spirit world. This is a situation that is very different to most parts of the 'Two-Thirds World' that has been experiencing phenomenal church growth.

Deliverance. At the time of writing, while I have no doubts about children needing a specific prayer ministry to set them free from demonic pressure and activity, I do have some doubts about children themselves being involved in any kind of deliverance ministry. I would certainly not encourage it, unless with an experienced adult. At the same time, I am reluctant to teach children to fear the devil, who is not the 'opposite of God'. He is an enemy to 'respect' and take seriously, but he is, after all, only a fallen angel, who does not have infinite powers.

It would seem reasonable to suppose that if a child seeking to minister to another child discerned some kind of demonic presence:

- the Father would not give them that discernment unless He would also equip them with the means to bring release to the other child;

- their purity and simplicity of faith might in some ways be more effective than an adult, rational faith; and

- the child might be taught to seek adult partnership before embarking on any kind of deliverance ministry.

Gifts – a mark of spirituality? It seems that some Christians put too high a value on the gifts of the Holy Spirit. Others have written in more detail about the various scriptural words used. One of the most helpful to me as a young Christian was the term 'gracelets' – these were manifestations of grace.They are gifts from God, and therefore precious. They are, however, gifts of grace and not rewards – they are no indication of 'spiritual status', as many adults seem to regard them. St Paul tells us that they are temporary, and imperfect this side of heaven (1 Cor. 13:8–10). They are not the things which will be taken into heaven – faith, hope and love are the things which are of most importance.

Someone has said that character must match gifting, yet this is no condition for receiving the Spirit. I remember being taught that gifts say more about the giver than the receiver. God gives wonderful gifts to His children, and with them He gives responsibility for their use. They are no short cut to maturity. Many an adult (and church fellowship) who has enjoyed much use of spiritual gifts has 'fallen from grace'. Much publicised examples from the Church in the United States have shown that some even have a spiritual ministry while living an immoral life! (Romans 11:29 may be an appropriate Scripture on this point.) This helps me to keep this whole topic in perspective, whether with children or with adults. The experience of the Spirit is a tool, given by God for service. The focus is not to be on the tools, but on the object that is crafted by them – or, in this case, the One who is glorified through them, Jesus Christ, our Lord.

Children ministering. 'Kids are kids.' From our observations, the reception of God's power and the use of supernatural gifts do not necessarily indicate maturity in any way. It seems that God simply comes in answer to simple childlike faith – as applauded by Jesus Himself. This can be most disconcerting for adults, who see children apparently ministering a powerful expression of God's power one minute, and then fighting or doing some other childish thing the next! Children do not always understand the significance or importance of some of these gifts. A child might casually report a picture or vision God has given, which subsequently has a powerful effect on a church or individual. Chris Leach gives an example of a four-year-old girl who, in effect, prophesied that a woman in the congregation was to have twins! The child did not say, 'The Lord is telling me . . .' or 'I believe that you are going to have twins . . .' Rather, she said it in a matter-of-fact way that would perhaps normally be dismissed as childish fantasy. [6]

Children sometimes pray briefly for someone's healing, and move on quickly to the next person, because they simply expect God to answer their prayer just like that! However, in my experience it is often because they need training in prayer, on how to 'wait on God', how to engage with the Holy Spirit and respond to His leading. The exciting thing is that children are quick to learn these things and put them into practice, even if their concentration sometimes lasts for only a very short time.

I do not expect children to minister like adults, though I expect adults to 'model' procedure and practice for children to copy. Children are unlikely to undertake 'inner healing', and I would not expect it. Apart from my earlier comments about deliverance (not actually a 'gift' of the Spirit anyway), I see no spiritual charismata that children are unable to receive, as and when the Holy Spirit chooses to give it in response to a situation. God will use those who are open, available, willing to be used, and who have faith in God!

Faith and Understanding. We need to remember that as a child matures emotionally, intellectually and socially, so will his or her understanding of the gifts and power of God manifested through them. In the meantime, we must not use adult criteria to measure the spirituality of children. We must, however, give them the benefit of our maturity and wisdom as they are apprenticed in the things of God. This should not be restrictive, and we need continually to take risks, as we allow them to learn by their own experience, and not just ours! Clearly, we do not want them to be harmed, but human experience reminds that 'getting one's fingers burnt' can be a good learning experience! We learn a lot by trying and making mistakes.

Many adults argue for the necessity to understand the things of God before one can experience/use them. Whilst this most certainly is the goal, it cannot be a condition of receiving and/or using a grace of God. To use this as an excuse for denying children what God would give them is unjust, to say the least. There are many things adults do not understand, but we still receive them 'by faith'. That faith is the child's greatest quality, and that is why they so often receive these things long before they understand them or even recognise them. For instance, after teaching, many children discover they have often had pictures or visions from God – they just didn't realise it. Others have been using 'funny words' for years when they prayed to God, without realising they were speaking in tongues.

Kingdom understanding. Another concept to bear in mind concerns a 'Kingdom' understanding of the purpose of salvation.

Howard Snyder says: 'Jesus' mission was to tell the good news of the kingdom, show what the kingdom was like, demonstrate its works, tell how to enter it, and establish the messianic community in embryonic form. He died on the cross and rose again to defeat the kingdom of evil and bring in the age of the kingdom of God.'[7]

John Wimber in a book on the Kingdom of God says something very similar. I feel that the concept of the Kingdom is an important one, for this is what we are seeking to impart to our children.

The KINGDOM OF GOD is the Rule of God (the age to come) which has invaded the kingdom (rule) of Satan (this present evil age), and is the arena in which signs and wonders occur. They are the 'marks' (signs) of the Kingdom. Understanding about the Kingdom of God is fundamental to understanding the ministry of Jesus; the kingdom of Satan was his real enemy. There is a war on! Jesus was sent by God to shatter the strongholds of Satan. His one purpose was Satan's defeat.

Jesus accomplished this through his death, resurrection and ascension. This demonstrated who was the victor, but Satan is not yet cast out and will not be until Christ returns to establish his Kingdom for ever. The Church is God's army in the continual fight which goes on with Satan as she lives 'between the times'.[8]

In charismatic churches, children often miss out. They are not present when the supernatural is happening, and often have no experience of spiritual gifts. 'Ministry', for instance, often happens after the service in a distant corner for privacy, away from the children, who may 'spoil' it by their noise and 'insensitive' curiosity. Children often grow up learning about God's power in stories, but never experiencing it for themselves. No wonder many are seduced by the offer of supernatural power through the occult, when the Church seems to deny them the genuine article.

Words and works. Children need to be taught not just about the theory but about the practice of living in the Spirit. That, of course, is where so much of our children's ministry is weak. We teach children the truths of the Gospel (the words of Jesus), but do not lead them into doing the deeds of the Gospel (the works of Jesus). My appeal, therefore, is for the balance to be regained. Many of those who seek to read 'the signs of the times' believe that God is going to pour out the power of His Spirit on children and young people in such measure as we have not yet seen in Church history. Many of us believe that our role with children in the Church is to prepare and train them, so that they will be ready when God moves in sovereign power.

I believe there is a very strong case for children to be baptised, immersed, or released in the Holy Spirit, and to begin to minister in His power as soon as they are able.

5

Preparing the ground

The experience of the Spirit is part of the growth of the Christian disciple. To prepare a person to enter into this experience is rather like a farmer tilling the soil. The ground may have been ploughed to break it up some weeks earlier, but the preparation for sowing is tilling it, breaking it down even more into fine soil, into which the seed can drop, be covered and begin the germination process. This chapter concerns this stage of preparing the ground.

The process can take many weeks, even months, yet it can also take only hours. No two groups of children are the same. Those children's evangelists who have an itinerant ministry need to develop extreme sensitivity to the Holy Spirit, to know what stage has been reached by the children being taught. One can only begin where the children are, and take them as far as time and the programme allow. Those in a pastoral setting have obvious advantages.

There is a sense in which the experience of the Spirit's power is a spontaneous event. Jesus said, 'The wind blows wherever it pleases. You hear its sound, but you cannot tell where it comes from or where it is going. So it is with everyone born of the Spirit' (John 3:8). We are dealing with the sovereign Lord. He can and will move where He wills. In the recorded instances of the Spirit of God falling on people, supposedly out of the blue, there has in fact, in most cases, been some kind of preparation time – even if the recipients were largely unaware of it when it was happening. For instance, the group of school children who spontaneously received the gift of tongues in Singapore attended a Christian school, where there was a real emphasis on prayer.

We can prepare for such a spontaneous move of God in the same way as we prepare for the return of the Lord Jesus Christ. It is a general state of readiness and openness to the wind of the Spirit. We can also have a period of planned preparation, after which we can pray for children to receive the Holy Spirit. It is this kind of preparation that concerns me here.

Trinitarian teaching

It seems that more and more evangelists and children's workers have become aware of the deficiency in teaching about the Godhead. If adults find the concept of the Trinity hard to understand or explain, how much harder it is for children. Because junior-age children are concrete thinkers, and because of the desire to avoid the clichéd image of God the Father sitting on a cloud in the sky (heaven), teaching has been almost entirely centred on the person of Jesus Christ, particularly in the evangelical churches. Jesus is the incarnate Son of God – He was (and is) a real person, who experienced human birth, childhood, adolescence and manhood. Though we have no photograph or contemporary painting, it is not hard for us to imagine what He looked like. It is even possible for us to teach and help children to grasp the fact that Jesus was also God – not God looking like a person, or a person who became 'god-like', but God, who was there 'with God in the beginning' (John 1:1). But our teaching must become more biblical, whilst remembering the learning characteristics of primary-school-age children.

No one knows what God the Father looks like. 'No-one has seen the Father except the one who is from God' (John 6:46).

'God is Spirit,' Jesus said (John 4:24), but even though God is not a man, Jesus taught us to call Him 'Our father'. How important it is for children in these days of dysfunctional families to have a correct image of Father God. Rather than avoid the topic, we should be asking the Holy Spirit, the Teacher, to help us in the task.

Then, of course, we must teach that the Holy Spirit is also God. He, too, was 'in the beginning' (Gen. 1:2). Jesus said that when He went, He would send another just like Himself, who would be with us for ever. The Holy Spirit is even called the Spirit of Christ (Rom. 8:9). This Spirit is heard as the sound of a violent wind, and seen as flames of fire reminiscent of the burning bush that Moses saw (Acts 2:2,3; Exod. 3:2). When Jesus was baptised in the River Jordan, 'the Holy Spirit descended on Him in bodily form like a dove' (Luke 3:22). Yet Jesus never spoke of the Spirit as an 'it'. In the Gospel of John, over and over again Jesus refers to the Spirit as 'He'.

What do you find most difficult in teaching children about God?

What illustration have you used to help children understand the concept of the Trinity?
(Try using a cube, colouring each pair of adjacent faces a different colour. It is possible to hold the cube so that only two faces are visible at a time. Display the cube, moving it out of sight momentarily to change the visible sides, giving the illusion of displaying three different cubes. Then display the whole cube, rotating it so that all sides can be seen. With this illustration one can make the point that each person of the Godhead represents one way of 'seeing' the one God.)

We begin to realise that this person of the Godhead falls into that abstract dimension that is so hard for young children to grasp. Rather than go into great detail about what He is, I have found it a great help to talk about what He does. To illustrate this, one can give contemporary examples, but generally I explain and point out His work in the life of Jesus Himself, using simple points such as the following:

a. In order to do His work, Jesus was filled with the power of the Holy Spirit when He was baptised (Luke 3:21–2). Day by day He spent time in prayer – listening to Father God and doing what the Father told Him or showed Him (cf. John 5:19; 12:49–50; 14:31).

b. After His death and resurrection, Jesus returned to be with God the Father in heaven, but He sent the Holy Spirit to be with us for ever (John 15:26; 16:5–15).

c. Jesus wants us to follow His example – to be filled with the power of the Holy Spirit (Acts 1:8), to listen to God and to learn to hear His voice in our heart and mind. Then we can do what God wants us to do!

There are other teaching points from the life of Jesus which illustrate the working of the Spirit of God. It could be argued that Jesus manifested every gift of the Holy Spirit except tongues. For example, in the story of His encounter with Zacchaeus (Luke 19:1–10), Jesus seemed to receive a 'word of knowledge' as he passed through Jericho that if he looked up into this particular sycamore-fig tree, He would see a man called Zacchaeus. Then Jesus seemed to receive a 'word of wisdom', for his unusual reaction was to invite himself to the man's home ('for tea' as the children's songs have it). Was this a case of the Holy Spirit manifesting Himself through

Christ, or was it a case of the divinity of Jesus that meant He had these attributes in His own right? I am inclined towards the former viewpoint.

Moving on from the example of Jesus Himself, we can then expand some of the other biblical teaching about the Spirit's work in the Christian, in that God wants to equip every Christian for the tasks He has planned for us, so that God's family, the Church, can be all that God wants it to be (Eph. 4:11–16). This, I explain, is why Jesus sent the Holy Spirit.

Fruit and gifts

A full description of the work of the Holy Spirit must include the fact that He helps us to be what God wants us to be, as well as to do what God wants us to do. His work is to create in us the character of Jesus – 'He makes me more like Jesus', as one version of a family service creed puts it. St Paul describes these character traits as the 'fruit of the Spirit' (Gal. 5:22,23). There has been a lot of talk about the competition between fruit and gifts of the Spirit and, fortunately, a lot of teaching about the complementary nature of these two aspects of His work in the believer. Unhelpfully, there has also been some confusion by describing the fruit as gifts, too. It is important to point out to the children that the Bible teaches very clearly that it is the fruit of walking close to Jesus that matters in heaven – 'these three remain: faith, hope and love . . . ' (1 Cor. 13:13). Prophecies, tongues and the rest of the supernatural gifts will cease – there is no need for them in heaven! Why is this? St Paul tells us that we can have all these gifts and not keep close to Jesus. That must be true, because we can have them and not have the fruit of the Spirit of Jesus – especially love.

I was brought up to understand that apples grow on an apple tree because that is the nature of an apple tree. If the fruit does not grow, there is something wrong with the tree. Applying this illustration, the fruit of the Holy Spirit grows because that is the nature of a Holy Spirit tree – i.e. the Christian. This is in contrast to fruit of the sinful nature tree (cf. Gal. 5:16,19), which is quite the opposite. St Paul's exhortation is to 'live by the Spirit and you will not gratify the desires of the sinful nature' (Gal. 5:16). In other words, as we seek to live close to God, in obedience and faith, co-operating with the work of the Holy Spirit within us, we will see the fruit of the Spirit. We are not to strive after the fruit, rather we strive after the Spirit, who will glorify Jesus and make us more like Him. It is not that we should try and be more patient, for instance; rather we should seek to get (or keep) closer to Jesus and we will become more patient, for that is a consequence of the action. When we see that parts of the character of Jesus are lacking in us, there is something wrong with the tree – we need healing, perhaps, or we need to walk more closely with Jesus. We must not forget the warnings of Jesus Himself about branches that do not bear fruit (John 15:1–8)!

When it comes to children, we must realise that some of these character traits are not the norms for children, because they are immature, and are in the maturation process. Teaching about character is also a challenge, because it is not quite so exciting. We must seek to be balanced in our teaching, but it may be that in a pastoral situation, we can encourage each other to see the fruits of the Spirit whenever they are displayed. Such encouragement can really help things along!

Curiosity killed the cat

Curiosity is a wonderful tool in the hands of a teacher/leader. If it can be aroused in children, rather than being the trap that 'kills', a door of opportunity opens that is a thing of great value. Children are curious by nature, for that is how they learn. For many children, the Holy Spirit is, perhaps, the biggest mystery of the Trinity. The apostles did supernatural things, filled with the Holy Spirit, yet we live in an age when Satan has hijacked the supernatural. Children usually grow up learning about God's power in stories, but never experiencing it for themselves. When talking about the Holy Spirit, I have realised that most children have no frame of reference against which to test this information of a divine being who is a 'He', yet is portrayed as such varied things as fire, wind and a dove. I have come, therefore, to the realisation that children begin to understand when they have an experience of the Holy Spirit themselves.

It is this matter of *experience* that is so important, for the Spirit of God is primarily the person of the Godhead who *does* things. He is the one who gives power to do what Jesus wants us to do (while never forgetting He also helps us be what Jesus wants us to be). Yet for many children (and perhaps for many adults) their experience of the Christian faith is that one does not *do* much at all! Much of our children's work is cerebral, whereas they learn so much through experience. Children need to realise that God truly is the *living* God because of what He does, in and through us. If children have perhaps *seen* God the Spirit doing something, that sense of curiosity may be aroused, and many will be more receptive to the biblical teaching I have outlined earlier.

How, though, can we let children see the Holy Spirit at work? Many children's leaders find this area personally difficult, for they feel they have had little or no experience of their own. In many churches there is an understandable fear about the supernatural – and some of the more dramatic accounts of the 'Toronto Blessing' add to the fear of some! Scenes of children 'resting in the Spirit', laughing or crying can cause some to panic. Can we not teach children about the

Holy Spirit and give them an experience of God's power without such phenomena? We are rightly cautious about such things, for we are careful for our children. Yet I have to return to the teaching that Jesus gave which enables us to conclude that surely we can trust our heavenly Father to give *good* gifts to His children.

If 'Toronto' has not hit your church (as they say), or you are not a charismatic church, how can you give children an experience of the Spirit's power? If the adult members of the church have not shared the experience (and may not wish to do so), I would generally advise that unless God takes the initiative, the experience of children in the church should be a reflection of what God is doing in the adults.

However, to start with, one can take them where He is demonstrably at work. Members of a diocesan renewal group (or similar group within your denomination) may be able to offer good suggestions here. Let the children see healing ministry take place, let them hear tongues and prophecy. There may be giggles at new sights and sounds, but my experience is that children love to see God at work! This in itself is an education. However, be prepared for the children who want to know why such things can't happen in their church!

If you can't manage such a visit, you could consider viewing a suitable video. Such videos are still hard to find, because of the sensitive nature of times of prayer ministry. Even more rare are videos which have scenes of children ministering in, or receiving, the power of the Holy Spirit.[1]

However, I have found it even better to lead children into an actual experience of the Holy Spirit of their own after a minimal introduction, and then teach out of their experience. I will deal with such experiential learning in the next chapter.

The problem of adults

However, there are other issues which must continue to be addressed at this stage. For instance, if the vision for children to be included in what God is doing in the church is one shared by the leadership, and not just the children's workers, the question has to be asked, 'What about the other members of the congregation?' I have generally found that other itinerant children's workers share my experience, namely, that the children get the vision, their leaders get the vision, the leadership of the church gets the vision, but the process is stopped and the work of the Spirit seemingly quenched by other adult members of the church.

Draw up a short list of questions which may be used in a survey of adult opinion about children and the experience of the Holy Spirit's power.

Write down your anticipated response, and then check it with the actual response.

Bearing in mind the planning steps outlined in a previous chapter, what steps need to be taken, and how long may it take for significant change to occur?

The adult members of the church need to be prepared to receive what God gives to, and through, children. How can this be done? As is so often the case, those who need to hear the message are not present when it is being preached! I have previously commented on the publication of the 1988 *Children in the Way* report in the Church of England. To have children taking any kind of lead is generally a cultural aberration, because naturally we assume that matters of maturity, know-ledge and experience determine such things. Adults are therefore threatened when children manifest spiritual gifts, often in a matter-of-fact way, and miss the point made earlier that gifts are gifts – acts of grace by our heavenly Father, and the Spirit manifesting Himself in those who are open and available, with the capacity to speak or act in simple faith.

The majority of adults in this country have not experienced children responding to God in power – not even those from charismatic churches. Thus there is no frame of reference. Sometimes God intervenes, with a demonstration of divine power in which children are included, but often it is by careful and patient explanation and teaching that adult church members are helped to see what God wants to do in and through our younger brothers and sisters in Christ.

Parents

If there is a need for careful and patient preparation of ordinary adult members of the church to accept the partici-pation of children in things of the Holy Spirit, then how much more is the need of the parents. Of course, most parents will be among those adult members of the church, but many children are the sole representatives of their families in the congregation. Even if the church decides to move ahead in this area, other, non-church parents should also be advised of your intentions, for they have the prime responsibility for their children.

I have already mentioned some of the problems that can arise from non-Christian parents. One answer is to make relationship-building a priority in the family ministry of the church. Visiting the home of every child each week is one of the keys of 'success' in Bill Wilson's vast Metro Church in Brooklyn, New York, despite the huge amount of time needed for the task by the dedicated workers. The frequency of such visits should be determined locally. One or two a year might be a more realistic goal for many churches.

Visiting is one way to build relationships, but whether this is possible or not, most churches would benefit from creating and maintaining some kind of attractive, user-friendly news-sheet. I recently came across one such occasional news-sheet published by a church in the High Wycombe area.[2] It was obvious that this was not a 'preachy' paper, whose real intention was to convert the non-Christian parent. It began, '. . . we want you to realise that you matter, and your involvement with your children is an issue of the Kingdom of God. As such, therefore, those in leadership in the Church want to encourage you and help you in your role as parents.' I am not claiming that this is a perfect news-sheet, and it is too soon to judge its effectiveness, but it is an excellent attempt to harness the goodwill of all parents.

Other churches present a 'policy document' to all parents and those working with the children. This sets out the aims of the church and its children's ministry in a way that is easily read and does not require 'inside knowledge' of Christian jargon. If the home visits mentioned earlier are written into such a document, they will not be seen as intrusion into people's privacy. Both the policy document and the news-sheet mentioned above are ideal means of beginning to prepare the ground in the parents for the experience of the Holy Spirit in the children. It is not easy to explain spiritual matters to non-Christians, for, as St Paul says, 'The man without the Spirit does not accept the things that come from the Spirit of God, for they are foolishness to him, and he cannot understand them, because they are spiritually dis-cerned' (1 Cor. 2:14). This is no excuse not to try, however. My main point is that if we have tried to explain what we are doing, parents cannot complain that we are doing things with their children behind their backs and without their permission. It goes without saying, of course, that if a parent forbids their child from encountering God in this way, their wishes must be respected. God has His own ways of dealing with such situations. Our responsibility is to act wisely and prayerfully, continuing to pray and care for the child within the boundaries set by the parent. Where this would affect the other children, we may feel we must suggest they find another church. This is very extreme, however, and I would be more concerned for the well-being of the child.

How would you explain the experience of the Holy Spirit to non-Christian parents?

What kind of language would you use?

When so many non-Christians associate the supernatural with the occult, how can they be reassured that this is good, and is from God?

Integration

How charismatic is your church? This is not such an irrelevant question as it may at first seem. We are discussing the process of enabling children to experience the power of the Holy Spirit in their discipleship – to draw them nearer to Jesus and to equip them for their part in the 'good works, which God prepared in advance for us to do' (Eph. 2:10). If we are expecting the Spirit of God to manifest Himself through the children, there is a need to make some preparations for receiving the various revelations that God will give to them (visions, prophecies, words of knowledge, etc.). This needs to be set alongside the current practice of the adult church. Some churches that call themselves charismatic are suffering from the problems of being second or third generation congregations. It is not uncommon to find a charismatic church that has had none of the 'supernatural' gifts of the Spirit for many, many months.

This book is not the place to discuss the state of the adult church members. My desire is to stimulate a process in which careful thought is given for the place of the ministry *of* children, in addition to the ministry *to* children. Because this is an unknown factor, it is quite reasonable to suppose that the primary ministry of children will be to others in their group, i.e. children to children (and often including their leaders). There may be little expectation that children will be given 'words' in the context of adult worship, though children's leaders are asked to pass on any such revelations that they discern may be for the wider body of the church. In one church where this is the practice, it is usual for the leader to relay the message when the vicar agrees it may be for the adult congregation. It is their aim, however, to get to the point where the child feels able to speak in public.

One preacher told me of a small independent church near Derby, where it was not unusual to have a small child tug at his trouser leg whilst he was preaching, saying she had 'a word from the Lord'! What was more confounding was that often the word was an accurate one! I have asked many of those who have experience of children giving words in the context of all-age worship, and have come to the conclusion that the size of the congregation seems to have a bearing. It is in the smaller congregations that children are more able to share some kind of revelation without the filter process of going through a leader. Perhaps it is in the smaller congregation that there is more tolerance for the learning and practice of spiritual gifts – from adults as well as children. Perhaps it is in the smaller congregation where relationships are closer that a child (or adult) may be more easily corrected if the word is discerned to be wrong or incorrect in some way. The important issue is that there is a way in which all words are weighed by the leadership, and that training as well as encouragement is given. The openness and simple faith of a child does not mean that every revelation is right. They, too, 'prophesy in part', so there is no thought of idealising the ministry of children in any way. The preparation of the ground includes the expectation that children will have some part to play in God's direct communication to His people.

The ministry of children is not just restricted to the giving of words, however, and a later chapter will explore the healing ministry of children.

6

Introducing children to the Living God

I have mentioned the fact that children often have no frame of reference when it comes to thinking about the supernatural work of the Holy Spirit, and that personal experience has led me to see that to lead the children into an experience of the Holy Spirit can help them enormously in their understanding and receptivity. It is an activity I call

Creating the interest

My desire is to give the children a 'taste' of life in the power of the Spirit. This can happen formally, by means of a led exercise, or informally. In one church I had been speaking at the evening service, attended by a mixed congregation of adults and young people including some ten- to thirteen-year-olds from another local church. During the service some of those youngsters had responded to the invitation to give more of themselves to God and receive from Him. Two girls were among the handful who stepped forward for prayer. As I talked with each of them, I came to the conclusion that one of them had come forward 'for the ride' – in other words she was really there to support her friend, and not for any real desire for herself. Nevertheless, I prayed for them both, asking God to come in power upon them, whilst not actually believing it for both.

After the service there was further ministry as we prayed for various people who requested it. One of these was a woman with a back complaint who happened to be the group leader of the two girls. The two were watching as we prayed for the lady, who soon fell to the ground under the power of the Holy Spirit. As she lay there and we continued to pray for her, I called both girls over and asked to them to stretch out their hands over their leader and pray for her, watching what God was doing. I did not expect much more to happen, but I am of the opinion that if God is at work, it is a good idea to join in, where possible! What I did not expect was that both girls spontaneously found themselves speaking in tongues as they prayed, and that God met powerfully with both of them. As a bonus, the lady's back was much better when she eventually rose to her feet, and I am sure they had a lot to talk about as they returned home! This encouraged me to adopt the practice of involving children (and others) in similar situations, and time and time again I have seen them receive from God themselves.

However, this kind of thing may not yet happen in your church, and you may wish to have some special activity to enable it to do so. I would like to suggest two such activities that I have found to be most helpful. Although they have been adapted and changed over the years, I am most grateful to my friend Graeme Young who suggested them.

Pictures. 'In the last days, God says, I will pour out my Spirit on all people. Your sons and your daughters will prophesy, your young men will see visions, your old men will dream dreams. Even on my servants, both men and women, I will pour out my Spirit in those days, and they will prophesy.' These are the words of the prophet Joel, from the fourth or fifth century BC, quoted by St Peter on the day of Pentecost (Acts 2:17–18). Most readers of the Bible would agree that

God often spoke to people through dreams and visions. For example, the Magi were warned not to return to Herod in a dream (Matt. 2:12), and the Lord called to Ananias in a vision to be part of the forming of Saul as the apostle he was to be (Acts 9:10). 'Pictures' is a more accessible word for 'visions', without taking away any of the meaning or the mystery. It would seem that the prophet Jeremiah began his training in prophetic ministry through pictures: 'What do you see, Jeremiah?' (Jer. 1:11,13).

Why does God speak to us in pictures? I have asked this question many times. Children readily understand that it is easier to remember a picture, and that a picture is 'worth a thousand words'. God has so much to say to help us, and to fulfil. His purposes for us. God uses pictures as one means of 'speaking'. With this kind of background explanation, I ask if the children would like to take part in an experiment to see what it is like to receive a picture from God. Most children respond immediately, because any opportunity to *do* something is better than sitting and just listening! I go on to explain what we are going to do and how I am going to lead it. Only then do I give the actual invitation to take part. I give permission for any who wish just to watch, and in order to emphasise that this is perfectly acceptable, I usually invite any who do opt out to join me in praying for the others from where they are. The only rule is that they do not spoil it for the others.

I invite the children to stand, on the understanding that it seems we are often more receptive and able to concentrate better if we are standing. I suggest that the children cup their hands, as a picture in itself that they are willing to receive from Father God. I add that of course God will not place a picture actually in their hands – it is rather a kind of body language that says to God 'I'm ready to receive.' I suggest they close their eyes, as it is easier, at first, to receive a picture in our minds if we have closed eyes. I then pray a simple and brief prayer, thanking God that He speaks through pictures, and ask Him to come, by the Holy Spirit, and give the children a picture with a meaning. I explain all this before I do it, including the fact that I will then continue to pray quietly, holding out my hand over the children as I watch to see what God is doing. I explain that there is no 'magic' in stretching out my hand, rather it is a way of helping me to concentrate on the business of praying for the Spirit to come. If the children are familiar with the gift of tongues, I add that I may be doing that quietly.

I explain that different people have different kinds of picture. Some see 'snapshots', others see 'videos' where some action is taking place. Some don't 'see' a picture, but receive an impression or a thought in their minds. Some see colours and shapes without knowing what they are, and some see words. I also say that some don't see any kind of picture, and that is why I call it an experiment to see what it is like to receive a picture from God.

As soon as the children think they have a picture, I ask them to sit down and draw what they have 'seen' on a piece of paper provided for the purpose. I continue to pray for those still standing, saying that if they feel dizzy, it is quite all right to open their eyes briefly to regain their balance, and then continue to wait. If there are one or two other leaders present, they are briefed to give special prayer to any who seem to be standing for a long time. If necessary they can talk quietly to the child to see what they felt was happening, and to see if they discern any kind of spiritual blockage that needs pastoral action. Generally speaking, I reassure those who don't seem to get anything that it may simply be the fact that God has something else for us – maybe even the interpretation of someone else's picture. I don't display great disappointment or put any unfair 'blame' on a child who didn't receive a picture. The fact is that experience shows that most children *do* get a picture of some kind, even more than the proportion of adults doing a similar 'experiment'.

The next stage is to share the pictures. Ideally, each child should be encouraged to share what they have put on their sheet of paper. This is dependent on the size of group. If necessary, divide into smaller groups, each with a leader, and have each child share in the small group.

The 'experiment' is more about receiving pictures than learning about interpretation, for this is a 'taste of the Spirit's work'. However, I do ask the children if they know the meaning of their picture, and I am often surprised by the answers I receive. It is important to teach about 'meanings' rather than literal representations. Just as Jesus told word pictures with a meaning (parables), so it is that the pictures we receive are generally pictures with a meaning. For instance, Jeremiah's picture of an almond branch did not mean that God was going to do something with an actual almond branch! In that case it was a play on words, for the Hebrew word for almond was similar to the one for 'watching', and God said, 'You have seen correctly, for I am watching to see that my word is fulfilled' (Jer. 1:11,12). Thus, if a child has a picture of the pony she has always wanted, it may not necessarily mean that God is going to give her her heart's desire. Such a situation needs sensitive handling, helping the child to see what the pony may represent.

Do not attempt to interpret every picture by giving them adult concepts, or by attempting to connect them all together like a large mural. At this stage I let them stand as they are. An important part of the 'experiment' is to talk about the pictures, because if God speaks through a picture, it is important to 'deliver the message'. Children learn that a picture may be for themselves or for others. Rather puzzlingly, they may not be for now or the immediate future, either! I emphasise that such things are part of the mystery of God.

The thing I have observed over and over again in this 'experiment' is that children soon begin to realise that the pictures they give are not ones they would have given if I had simply asked them to draw me a picture! They learn that these pictures are 'given', that they are revealed by God. This is especially so when several children see that they have been given a similar picture without copying or getting ideas from anyone else. There is a spiritual understanding that God is not the product of our imagination, that He is real and He is outside of us as well as in us.

As children learn what it is like to have pictures from God, they are more likely to recognise it when God 'does it for real'. In this particular use of this 'experiment,' they are much more open to wanting to know more about the power of the Holy Spirit!

Hands-on praying.   The second exercise which I use to introduce children to the work of the Spirit of God is a way of introducing children to one method of prayer ministry. It was introduced to me as 'hands-on praying', but a fellow Church Army officer soon dubbed it 'drainpiping'.

I felt God tell me to do this exercise during an evangelistic Holiday Club. I was not at all sure about this, as I felt that the children needed to be somewhat committed before they could do it properly. However, I felt God's prompting was insistent, and so I obeyed. There was a lot of the usual giggling (children are not used to doing things like this) and some quiet prayer, but there was no great miracle that I could see. However, just before the Sunday morning family service I was beckoned over by a lady I had not seen before. She was seated on the front row (which obviously showed she was not a regular) and was accompanied by five or six children. 'The children all enjoyed your Holiday Club,' she said. 'We nearly didn't come this morning because the youngest was really ill before.' She pointed at the small child sitting with a big grin on her face. The lady continued, 'The others said, "We know what to do, Mum," and did your hands-on praying. And look, it worked – she's as right as rain!'

I make no claims for this incident. As far as I know there was no great commitment to Christ, and the family did not start to come regularly to church. Yet I do believe that it was God's doing, and that in His economy of things, it will bear greater fruit.

But what is this method, and how does it 'work'? The principle is simple. A group of children (with or without a leader) gather round someone who wishes to receive prayer. Each pray-er stretches one hand towards heaven, because it is God's love and God's power that brings healing. Graeme Young reminds us that Jesus said, 'The kingdom of God is at hand (is near)' (e.g. Mark 1:15). It is within reach, as it were. The hand raised to heaven is a symbol of our reaching to heaven to take what is there for the person for whom we are praying.

Because God chooses to use people like us who love Him and love others, we are the channels of His healing love and power, and so we stretch our other hand towards the person or lay it gently on them, as a reminder that God wants His love and power to flow through us because of our love and obedience. After waiting a moment or two to 'get in touch with heaven', a simple prayer is prayed, inviting the Holy Spirit to come on the person for whom we are praying. I encourage the pray-ers to keep their eyes open and watch to see if they get any clues about what God may be doing. This in itself is a novelty, as children are continually told to close their eyes when they pray! I explain to the children that if our arms get tired we can change them round! If they still get tired we can lower them. I do find that most children persist, however.

Meanwhile, I invite the person requiring prayer to stand or sit with eyes closed and hands cupped. Again, I explain that closed eyes mean we can concentrate on what may be happening within us, and that cupped hands are part of the body language that tells God and the pray-ers we are ready to receive. I always ensure that the children understand that healing means being made more whole. This means that we do not have to have something very wrong with us to receive God's healing, for all of us need to be made more whole, more and more!

These are the basic principles of hands-on praying. There are other things that may be added. Children, for instance, often want to know what to pray. I realise that I have integrated some of the principles of healing prayer learnt from John Wimber and the Vineyard churches, which makes it accessible even to children. For instance, I explain that because we are not doctors, and because we can trust Father God to do what is best, we do not need to pray clever prayers. I suggest that someone starts off by saying a simple thank-you prayer for the person, mentioning the felt need (if the child has expressed one) requiring God's healing touch, and concluding with the simple invitation to the Holy Spirit to come on the person in power. The others are invited to contribute in prayer, but only after listening to see if they know what God has for the person. In other words, they don't have to fill up a silence with words, though they are encouraged to continue praying quietly as they watch. I help them to be ready to give a Bible verse, if God reminds them of one, or to pray a prayer. If we have already talked about pictures, I say that a picture might 'pop' into their mind. If so, they should describe it, in case it means something to the person being prayed for. They should then pray about the picture –

it might be God showing exactly what to pray about! In other circumstances (for hands-on praying is not restricted to being simply an introduction to the Spirit's work), if they have the gift of tongues, I encourage them to use it quietly, realising that sometimes they might then be given the interpretation to those tongues.

After a short while I encourage them to ask if anything is happening. Sometimes the person can answer, but sometimes not. Children learn that we need to wait for God to move, as we continue to pray. I am not surprised by giggles and nervous laughter at first. However, if I feel that the children are being rather silly, I suggest we don't continue, as it does not honour God and it is not loving the person wanting prayer.

The other thing that children most often want to know is when to stop! I generally tell the children to stop when they have finished, or think that God has done what He wants to do, and give God the praise for His goodness and loving kindness.

When hands-on praying is part of normal ministry with children, I explain that we can pray again some time if there is still a need. Sometimes a person needs several such times of prayer. Children can learn to do this naturally.

Again, experience has shown over and over again that when children have had an experience of the supernatural, they are much more open to knowing more! Having had a taste of the Spirit's work, we may then be ready to provide an opportunity for those who wish to be more useful to God in the power of the Holy Spirit.

Who, when and how?

It is helpful to start with a group of children who want to go on with God. Much energy might be expended persuading the reluctant kids to take God seriously. Invite those who wish to experience more and know God better – the element of choice is often missing in children's ministry. Be aware, though, that the 'pain in the neck' children might be simply bored with hearing the same stuff over and over again. The opportunity to do things for God may be Gospel (Good News) for them!

The 'special event', a parish weekend or Praise Party, etc., might be the best time to seek God to move, just as an evangelistic mission is frequently the occasion for evangelistic response. It may be an event to which parents are invited, and in which they are involved. There should be no hint that this is for the 'A'-class Christians only! That mistake was made too much in the early days of charismatic renewal amongst adults, with disastrous results. All children are equally loved by God, whether or not they are ready to receive this particular experience. Every effort should be made to ensure this is known and felt by the children.

Some churches make good use of *Young Saints* – a six-week course for junior-age children on living in the power of the Spirit.[1] Robyn Barnett, children's worker at St Stephen's, East Twickenham, uses the material as an integral part of her programme for children in the church. She runs the course twice a year, preceded by what she initially called a 'Family Tea', though she has since dropped that title because parents felt their children were more motivated by the food! She writes, 'Beforehand I'll have an "open evening" for parents to attend, at my house, to explain the biblical principles for encouraging our children in this area, what the format of the "Family Tea" will be, and the material in the *Young Saints* course. Then, if they think their child is ready and happy to make this step and would like to come, they can encourage them to do so.'

A problem Robyn encountered was when parents expressed

concern that the event was initially advertised in the children's groups, rather than solely to parents for them to decide. Parents found themselves under pressure from their children when they hadn't yet worked things out for themselves. Personally, I find this an interesting issue, because I am so aware that adults always make decisions for the children. I am too aware of children being pushed into things by eager parents who, naturally, want the best for their children. Unfortunately, the children don't always agree, and that brings problems for the leaders of the event concerned!

> What do you think? Should parents decide for their children, or should children be helped to take the initiative, bearing in mind that they are under the authority of their parents?
>
> How would you advertise such an event?

Making the connection. Having prepared the ground, and realised the readiness of children to receive from God, how do we proceed? On what basis do I approach this matter?

For my part, I believe the authority of Scripture and the willingness of our Father God to 'give the Holy Spirit to those who ask Him' (Luke 11:13).

I make no presumptions on the sovereignty of God, but my understanding of Scripture, my experience and my faith lead me to expect God to move in power in our midst.

In my explanations I use language that is appropriate to children, without being babyish, and often end with the desire of the Holy Spirit, in my words, to make us more useful to God.

Often, I explain possible phenomena that children may

experience themselves or see in others (shaking, resting in the spirit, laughing, crying, etc.), but emphasise that many people experience none of these when they receive. This is a slightly difficult area, because I am only too aware that in such an explanation I may be 'programming' a response from children who may wish to please me! Others prefer not to give any such explanation until it happens. I offer more general advice on ministering to children in chapter 10.

Doing the stuff!   These are the five steps of receiving that I use with adults and children alike! (It is only the wording that changes slightly.)

1. A clean heart, or Getting right with God (Psalm 24:4). If children are to be filled with the Holy Spirit, they need to be clean inside. I offer various ways of doing this, seeking the inspiration of the Holy Spirit as to which way is appropriate now. Occasionally it may be done in pairs, confessing sins to each other. Often it is done in private, with children told to find a quiet space in which to clear things with God. Alternatively, it may be done liturgically, using one of the confessional prayers of the church. I find that children have no difficulty with this step, and know precisely what it is about.

2. Ask (Luke 11:9). My own practice is to do the asking in two stages. Stage one is where I pray for and over the children, assisted by other leaders or parents. I thank the Father for the opportunity, and ask the Holy Spirit to come in power. I ask for angelic protection against any action by the enemy, and continue to pray quietly in tongues. (I have already explained to the children that is what I am doing, so that they can keep their eyes closed and not be concerned about me!) Stage two is when the children ask God to fill them. I feel strongly that children should ask for themselves when they are ready, and

that they should ask out loud. I explain that this is rather like a wedding service, when the bride and groom each say their response out loud, not just in their minds, because their response is witnessed by the congregation. I explain that it does not matter if two or more speak at once, for they are not speaking to each other, but to God, who can hear millions of people in hundreds of different languages all at once!

If they have been instructed about the gift of tongues, I suggest that they might ask for this gift at the same time, if they wish. Again, it is their decision, and not mine, and no pressure is put on the child about this.

3. Receive, or Let go and Wait (Acts 1:4,8). This is the 'risky' part! Having asked, we wait for God to come in power. Sometimes He is swift and powerful in His coming. At other times He is gentle and takes His time. I do not know why He does it differently, He just does. David Walters writes,

> We instruct the youngsters and adults to be quiet and still before the Lord. We ask them to get their minds off everything except the Lord, open themselves up, and ask the Holy Spirit to come and possess them. That can be a little scary for some people. People think of demon possession, but not Holy Spirit possession. They think of 'having the Holy Spirit', but not the Holy Spirit having them. As we bring them to the place of faith, God always moves. [2]

4. Worship (Acts 2:8,11b). When the children believe God has begun to answer their prayer, they are encouraged to thank Him for what He has done and simply to worship Him. If they have asked for the gift of tongues, I encourage them to speak or sing out in words the Holy Spirit gives them. In my prior explanation I say that I will be praying in tongues for

them, and that when the Spirit begins to move I shall sing in tongues. Then, if and when they feel they are ready to release that gift, they can make their first sounds along with mine, if they wish. This enables some children to overcome that self-conscious feeling.

5. A daily top-up, or Post-operative instruction (Eph. 5:18; 2 Pet. 3:18)! 'The baptism in the Spirit is a filling station, not a parking lot!' an American preacher said. The Bible teaches that we must continue to ask God to fill us again and again with His Holy Spirit. I normally explain that when God fills us for the first time, we are so full that as we go about our daily lives, and 'bump' into people and situations, some of the Spirit gets spilt! As we set ourselves to live for Jesus, we 'give away' more of the Spirit in us, and so we need to come back to God for more. I explain that we probably won't feel the same feelings as the first time, and that we don't need a special meeting to do it; rather it becomes a normal part of our daily routine of prayer and waiting on God. I also add that whenever we are to do something special for God, it is a good idea to get someone else to pray for us for an appropriate special 'top-up'!

What if nothing happens?

I say to you: 'Ask and it will be given to you; seek and you will find; knock and the door will be opened to you. For everyone who asks receives; he who seeks finds; and to him who knocks, the door will be opened. Which of you fathers, if your son asks for a fish, will give him a snake instead? Or if he asks for an egg, will give him a scorpion? If you then, though you are evil, know how to give good gifts to your children, how much more will your Father in heaven give the Holy Spirit to those who ask him!' (Luke 11:9–13).

But what if nothing happens, or nothing appears to happen? Do we claim the Bible verse in which Jesus said, 'Whatever you ask for in prayer, believe that you have received it, and it will be yours' (Mark 11:24)? I believe we often do a lot of damage to young hearts when we claim 'by faith' that something has happened, when it hasn't. This can be sheer pretence. When it comes to the experience of being filled with the Holy Spirit, I believe one knows if it has happened or not – the child will know. The question is, if it has not happened, why not?

There may be several reasons, each of which needs sensitive pastoral care and action. It may be:

- because we have tried to rush things, and not given God enough time to do the work at His pace, and not ours;
- because there is some kind of unconfessed sin and/or the child has not yet received Jesus as Lord and Saviour;
- because there is some kind of emotional/spiritual blockage that needs counselling – possibly even deliverance (we have discussed earlier the possibility of a child being under demonic pressure). Sometimes a little more 'prayer power' of one or two leaders praying over the child will shift such a blockage!
- because the time is not right. God does not always do things as and when we expect; the Bible teaches that sometimes prayer is persistent persuasion! (See Luke 11:5–13). There is an element of mystery in this, in the same way that some are healed and others are not. We have to trust that God knows best. We must avoid making this the excuse for some other reason why the child has not received from God. In my experience this particular reason is actually not very common.
- because the child is not sincere in the matter. Perhaps he/she is doing it to please a friend, a parent – or even you, as the leader!

Finally, may I plead the following two simple points:

- Do not pressurise the children! There is the danger of enthusiastic leaders making kids feel guilty if they do not respond/react/receive as the leader expects.
- Be 'laid back' about the whole matter, whilst at the same time enthusiastic and convinced of the truth and importance of this anointing from God.

7

Let's start at the very beginning – children coming to faith

I never knew about 'giving my life to Christ' until I was a teenager. I was baptised, confirmed and went to church weekly – after all, I was in the choir. I was religious and believed in God. I knew I wasn't a good Christian, but I knew I wasn't a bad one, either! My earliest memories of Sunday School were of finding I could come home with more money that I took. I learnt a trick of putting my hand in the collecting bag with my threepenny bit, dropping the coin, but taking a quick grab at what was already there. Often I came out with a sixpence, but more often it was a penny or two. My dad put me right when he found me digging up my hoard at the foot of a tree in the churchyard. He never talked about it again, but I guess it must have disappointed him. The remarkable thing is that, like telling lies, no one taught me how to do it! I learnt how to steal all by myself! I never knowingly stole again, except, of course, in copying friends' records on to tape. But then, I could easily justify that kind of action – people do it all the time, don't they? Anyway, apart from a hot temper, a vocabulary of swear-words and a repertoire of dirty jokes I was a pretty decent bloke.

It all changed, of course, when a friend 'went religious',

and began the process of bringing me to the point when I knew beyond a shadow of a doubt that Jesus was my Saviour, and that I was safe in Him, through the forgiveness of my sins and the gift of eternal life. Thus at the age of nineteen I had my 'conversion experience'. At first, I thought that everything I had previously been taught was wrong, and that this was the real beginning – I was a 'born-again Christian'. However, I now interpret those events as the time when I took possession of all that had been promised me at my baptism, and to which I assented at my confirmation.

Of course, I am an Anglican – a member of the Church of England. For many, the issue of baptism and confirmation will at once brand me as either 'sound' or 'unsound', depending on one's churchmanship. However, God called me to be an evangelist in the Church very soon after my 'conversion', and I joined the Church Army, a society of evangelists within the Church of England. After three years' theological and practical training, in December 1971 I became a Church Army Captain and was admitted by the Archbishop of Canterbury to the office of Evangelist in the Church. Since that time I have had the privilege of leading hundreds to Christ, both children and adults. I have learnt a little of what that means in the different styles of churchmanship within the Church of England, whilst at heart being a convinced evangelical. Although terminology and words differ, and practice and interpretation might vary according to the situation in which I found myself working, the process was much the same, whether I was evangelising children or adults. What did flummox me was the frequent occurrence of children (especially) who kept responding to the invitation to give their lives to Christ. Like many other evangelists I was torn between saying, 'You don't need to do this again, because you've already given your heart to Jesus', and 'All those other times have been a kind of "dress-rehearsal" – now this is the real thing!' I was also aware of the number whose faith seemed to 'fade away'. I couldn't keep up correspondence with many – and I marvel at the number of evangelists who seem able to do so – but I rather suspect that many were subsequently lost to the Church (though not to Christ, I believe).

When God began to direct my ministry more specifically to children and young people, I began to ask myself hard questions, and to challenge some of my assumptions.

- How do children come to faith? Are they just like adults, or is there some other process by which they draw near to God and come to know Him and love Him?
- On what basis do we seek to evangelise children?
- When children (and some adults) give their lives to Christ more than once, at what point are they 'born again'?
- What about the rest of the family – how important is the home environment?

I must openly confess that I am no theologian – I am a practitioner. The word 'theology' frightens many people, for we have the image of sterile writing that is unintelligible to most of us, and seems to lack any sense of faith or good news! Add to this the stereotypes of theologians as dull boffins who use big words and are totally out of touch with normal people, and one sees the problem theologians have in public relations! Many shy away from the subject, appealing to a simple faith. Indeed, in a simple sense, all Christians are meant to be theologians as we read and study God's Word, the Bible. As a practitioner, I have sought to understand what the Bible says, and I have tried to listen to and understand the insights of others who seek after truth. I have weighed these against my own experiences, and tried to find the interpretation that helps me to function as a disciple, as an evangelist and as a children's worker. I have to say that what

I have discovered in these last few years has revolutionised my ministry, both to adults and to children. I am not attempting to give the definitive understanding of how children come to faith. Rather I am sharing the insights I have gained that have given me inspiration and hope in the ministry God has given me.

Whether or not we realise it, our theology of children determines our practice, just as much as the values examined in an earlier chapter.

Differing viewpoints

It may be helpful to give a summary of some of the different viewpoints on this matter of the spiritual status of children. Many children's workers don't realise there are differences and are either delighted or dismayed to find there are! Let us start with what might be termed the conservative evangelical viewpoint.

All children start life outside the Kingdom of God. From this approach children may be stated simply as being 'out of the Kingdom until they opt in'.[1] Traditional Bible passages about Adam and Eve's transgression in the garden and the subsequent Fall of man (Genesis 3) and St Paul's comparison of 'death through Adam, life through Christ' (Romans 5) – and other Scriptures about mankind being in rebellion against God – are applied equally to children as to adults, 'for *all* have sinned and fall short of the glory of God' (Rom. 3:23). The New Testament does not seem to differentiate between adults and children. Therefore, if there is no repentance and forgiveness, then the child is bound for hell. Of course, there is the acknowledgment that there is an 'age of accountability', when a child is old enough to know the difference between right and wrong. However, there is a lot of uncertainty as to

91

when this occurs. Can a child truly repent of his or her sins at the age of three or four, as many have claimed from personal experience? Is the wilful disobedience of an infant really 'sin', or is it the natural self-assertion of an immature human being? If a child dies before making such a response to Christ, is he or she bound for hell? The reality of hell, which may be defined as a 'Christ-less eternity', and the sure and certain hope of heaven is the black and white issue for this approach. The urgency of evangelism inspired by this view has been commendable, but it has resulted in confusion by many children who seem to be converted many times.

R. Hudson-Pope, a much respected children's evangelist of former years, gave the following outline which has been the hallmark of this approach for many, including the equally respected international Child Evangelism Fellowship. The outline is based on Matthew 18:1–14 (and depends on the King James version for its exegesis).

1. Children are very precious.

2. Children are lost.

3. Children have gone astray.

4. Children are perishing.

5. Children can be caused to stumble.

6. Children can believe in Jesus.[2]

It is the black and white statements of this approach that give me most cause for concern. 'Children are lost . . . Children are perishing'. All children are treated in the same manner, yet there are many adults who testify that there was never a time when they did not know and love Jesus. The problem I associate with this approach is that it is very 'event-orientated', and the event is the precise moment 'I give my life to Christ' (or whatever expression is used). Thus some parents will say of their primary-school-age children, 'Mary is saved, John isn't, but we're not sure about Pat.' Their statements are based on whether the child has made a conscious decision for Christ. The behaviour of all three children may be identical – they are all normal children, sometimes behaving in a Christian way and sometimes not – but their eternal destiny is based on the vocalised prayer of commitment.

The late Bishop Cuthbert Bardsley, in whose diocese of Coventry I served the early years of my ministry, married when he was in his sixties. He was an enthusiast for marriage and how it illustrated our relationship with Christ. I don't *think* I'm married,' he would say, his voice booming out from the pulpit, 'I *know* I'm married!' He was speaking of one of the greatest contributions of the evangelical wing of the Church – that of the assurance of faith. The Christian can say, 'I know' rather than, 'I hope so.' But every analogy has its weaknesses, and in these days of marriage breakdown we can see it all too easily. It seems to be clear either that many people who get married are not truly in love with their spouse, or that love quickly fades with the passage of time. Thus the act of commitment in itself is no guarantee. On the other hand, marriage is the culmination of a process of growing love and commitment. Love was there before the wedding. The ceremony was the witnessed commitment that took it a stage further.

But how does this relate to children? It simply highlights an approach that is centred around our response to Christ, and the point at which a person is born again. Perhaps it may be fairer to say that those who hold this viewpoint treat children as if they are unconverted until they see the evidence.

Jesus said, 'I tell you the truth, no one can see the kingdom of God unless he is born again . . . no-one can enter the kingdom of God unless he is born of water and the Spirit . . .' (John 3:3,5). But these words of Jesus must be weighed against His other sayings, one of which is at the heart of the next approach we shall consider.

All children belong to God. If the former position could be summarised as saying that children are out of the Kingdom until they opt in' then this approach says they are 'in the Kingdom until they opt out'.[3]

Jesus said, 'Let the little children come to me, for the kingdom of God belongs to such as these' (Mark 10:14). Scholars have debated what He meant by the phrase 'such as these', but those with this viewpoint interpret Jesus as actually meaning children.

The late John Inchley, another children's evangelist, was won to this position by the teaching of Dr W. H. Griffith-Thomas, an evangelical Anglican who, in the 1930s, was one of those who wrestled with the issues of spiritual accountability. St Paul says, 'Where there is no law, there is no transgression' (Rom. 4:15; 5:13). It follows, they say, that children and 'irresponsible persons' will be recipients of the free grace that comes through Christ's reconciling death on Calvary, until they deliberately refuse Him.

Those who hold this viewpoint see Mark 10:13–16 as a key passage, and from this draw two statements:

1. The kingdom belongs to children; that is why they come to Jesus.

2. Our approach is not the evangelism of those outside the kingdom, but the nurture of those within.

There is a danger of what is called universalism in this viewpoint. Are all children 'saved' – even the children of parents holding other faiths (and none)? A lady asked me, 'Is my son going to go to heaven then? He has never rejected Christ.' The 'child' was twenty-six years old, and had never accepted Christ either!

There are other questions that arise about when childhood ceases, and the definitions of childhood itself. Some might also apply the apparently logical thinking that says, 'If we keep them ignorant, they cannot reject Christ!' Others may feel in addition that this viewpoint does not take sin seriously, but this is not so. Those who hold this view simply point out that as a child grows in understanding, so will the 'awareness of the sinfulness of sin as the thing that God hates, in the light of the character and reality of Christ'.[4]

John Inchley was a wise man, and in my reading of him and my memories of him (he was still leading children's missions well past his retirement!) he was a man who had the heart of Jesus for children. Jesus did not put conditions on children – He welcomed all children, not just the repentant and believing ones. He did not tolerate them, He wanted them and made time for them. He said, 'Your Father in heaven is not willing that any of these little ones should be lost' (Matt. 18:14).

There are other schools of thought which add to a greater understanding of how children come to faith.

Faith development. This is the understanding gained by social scientists whose basis is not theological, in the sense that the Bible is not a source of their evidence. Rather, it has evolved through studies in developmental psychology, especially in child psychology, and comes from scientific observation and research. Some might wish to ignore it because of these factors. However, despite an unwillingness to accept all the claims of such a perspective without criticism, two major reports to the Church of England General Synod concerning children (*Children in the Way*, 1988, and *All God's Children?*, 1991) both acknowledged the value of the insights gained from developmentalists (as they are called). Two such scholars are frequently mentioned and quoted, John Westerhoff and James Fowler. Like many others, I sometimes have difficulty understanding their work mainly because of the words they use! This book is not the place to give an analysis of their work; it is sufficient to say that, despite similarities, their work is quite different: Westerhoff emphasises the relationship between religious education and the Christian community, while Fowler sees faith as an active commitment to the source of personal ultimate meaning – a personal faith that is not bound by religious commitment to a particular content of beliefs.

Many people seem able to understand Westerhoff's comparison of growth in faith and the growth of a tree. As a tree grows and develops its annual rings it changes – and those changes are gradual. It is not a better tree because it has grown, it is just different. He has identified four 'growth rings' which he describes as 'styles of faith' that develop usually during childhood and adolescence. These are generalisations and each style, he believes, is complete and valid for a person at that stage. Unlike some developmentalists, he does not specifically relate any of these stages to a particular age. He believes that one is able to move backwards and forwards between stages, according to one's spiritual growth, so that the needs of each stage are met accordingly.

The four 'styles' are as follows:

EXPERIENCED FAITH. This is about experiencing the actions of others and learning to trust and be trusted. The relationships within the family and with 'significant others' enable the child to explore and assess faith in action, which may or may not be Christian faith. The experienced faith becomes simply the norm.

AFFILIATIVE FAITH. As the child becomes aware of the community to which he or she belongs, there is a natural tendency to identify and act with others and develop a sense of belonging. The need to be accepted, wanted and valued by that community is characteristic of this stage. Junior-school-age children are particularly at this stage (though it can last for many years). Many children come to faith in Christ by meeting a Christian group (Sunday School or whatever). They like the group and want to belong, and if Jesus makes the difference, they are happy to take Him on board. This seems to me to be very similar to the 'household conversions' of the New Testament, and the tribal conversions that are reported from some Two-Thirds-World countries.

SEARCHING FAITH usually occurs later in adolescence, when there is a greater independence of spirit. In this third stage there is a period of doubt, questioning and experimentation with alternative understandings and traditions. Only then, it is argued, does one reach the stage of commitment to a personal faith.

When the needs of this stage have been adequately met, then one expands into what Westerhoff refers to as:

OWNED FAITH. In this category, one not only owns one's faith, but in a sense is owned by one's faith, in being willing to witness to one's faith with integrity. *All God's Children?* says, 'It is the end of a conversion experience which is usually "a long pilgrimage", although there can be times of sudden discovery within the process.'[5]

There are other viewpoints which could be explored, but these are sufficient. But what is it that has 'revolutionised my ministry, both to adults and to children', as I said earlier?

A way forward

I felt that I, too, could not identify with all the claims of the developmentalists – I had seen too many exceptions to the categories. I knew the assurance of salvation and the importance of coming to that point of 'knowing', and was convinced of the importance of the words of Jesus, 'the kingdom of God belongs to such as these'. As an Anglican, I wanted to understand the place and significance of baptism and the other 'rites of passage', as they are called, in it all. And so it was that I realised the significance of the fact that *salvation is a process*, and not an event. For most of my life I had been taught to place the importance on the time at which one was born again, and had lost sight of the fact that the Bible teaches that one can say, 'I have been saved' (e.g. Eph. 2:5), 'I am being saved' (e.g. Phil. 2:12) and 'I will be saved' (e.g. Matt. 24:13).

As a chaplain at Lee Abbey, a Christian holiday and conference centre in North Devon, I was struck by a series of epilogues led by a fellow chaplain, based on John Bunyan's famous classic, *Pilgrim's Progress*. I remember him asking the guests at what point Pilgrim was saved. Was it when he left the wicked city, or when he lost his burden at the cross, or when he crossed the river? This was my first clue to this most basic of understandings. The second was gained on reading a small book by Ron Buckland, in which he said, 'It is my belief that many people, including children, make decisions towards Christ. Rather than making a once-and-for-all decision to follow Christ, I see these gradual steps into dawning light becoming that radical reorientation of life called Christian discipleship. God alone knows the point at which a person is "saved".'[6]

When someone responds to the Gospel message, it does not matter whether it is the first or the twenty-first time they have done so! Rather than being concerned about when a person *has become* a Christian, it would seem more appropriate to talk of a person (a child or an adult) becoming *more* Christian with each step of response.

The Good News is that we can have an assurance that we are 'saved' by the witness of the Holy Spirit within – 'The Spirit himself testifies with our spirit that we are God's children' (Rom. 8:16). However, that is still not the end of the Christian 'journey', and we are encouraged over and over again to keep going and keep growing (see Phil. 2:12,13; Col. 2:6,7; 2 Pet. 3:18).

When it comes to children, I am no longer able to 'treat them all as if they are unsaved', for I know this not to be true. Many children have been prayed for before birth and ever since. They have grown up knowing and loving Jesus. That is not to say that they do not need evangelising, for they, and we, constantly need to hear the Good News that challenges our will and leads us to the point at which we yield our lives more and more to the Lordship of Christ. While training as a Church Army student, I remember being told, 'I can only give as much as I know of myself to as much as I know of God.' As I grow and live my life, both those dynamics change; there is, therefore, always more of me to give to the more I learn of Him.

My working 'definition' of the spiritual status of children is drawn from that little book that helped me so much:

All children begin with God, but unless an effective evangelistic or nurturing influence comes to bear on a child, he/she will move steadily away from God.

Ron Buckland goes on to say, 'It is a belongingness that may become rebellion. The desire to nurture that belonging, and to avoid that rebellion, propels us to urgent teaching and evangelism.'[7]

Consequences

There are several consequences of this understanding as far as children are concerned. First, whenever the Gospel message is proclaimed, I expect the Holy Spirit to be at work. On most occasions where it is appropriate, I seek to give an opportunity for my audience to respond. I am learning to trust the integrity of children, encouraging them to discern whether or not God is asking something of them, listening to the voice of the Spirit within. I do not expect that response to be always to say 'yes' to Jesus as a first time response. Rather, it may often be that yielding of the will, a 'turning back' when the child knows they have 'gone astray', albeit ever so slightly. Some children just simply want to love Jesus more, whilst others want more of Him.

When Dr Billy Graham, the world famous evangelist, gives an evangelistic, appeal at the end of one of his meetings, hundreds and thousands pour forward. He never claims that these have given their lives to Christ, even if that was the invitation. In the one-to-one counselling that follows, it soon becomes evident that people respond to the same message for many different reasons – that is the work of the Holy Spirit, as people hear different Good News from the same message. I remember one of his last visits to Earl's Court in London. His talk that evening was to my mind nothing out of the ordinary. The message and his invitation to respond at the end was very much directed at the adult audience. However, I was amazed to see the large numbers of young children who also poured forward – the Holy Spirit was talking to them, and they knew it.

My friend Graeme Young has summarised the responses that children may make in four 'T's, based on St Peter's reply to the question, 'Brethren, what shall we do?' Peter said, 'Repent and be baptised in the name of Jesus Christ for the forgiveness of your sins, and you will receive the gift of the Holy Spirit' (Acts 2:38). The four responses are: Turn, Trust, Tell out and Take in. After a brief explanation, Graeme asks children which of those responses they have already made, and which they feel God is asking them to make now.

Notice that we are talking about responses, not decisions. Many now share some of the anxieties about decision-orientated evangelism amongst children, and feel decidedly uncomfortable about looking for adult-type responses from children. Some seem to go even further, and feel that reaching and evangelising children is all about the non-manipulative planting of lasting impressions. Children are capable of far more than simply gaining these impressions, as many can testify. We cannot ignore the work of the Holy Spirit in children, although some may say this is no more than manipulation. I beg to differ, but acknowledge we are all entitled to our opinions, and each must come to a knowledge of the truth that God seems to reveal to us, even if it differs from my understanding! For me, the important thing is that I look for and encourage growth in faith, giving children opportunities to mark those steps along the way, in the same way that milestones tell us we are not in the same place we were, though neither are we at journey's end.

The second consequence concerns evangelistic literature. Even in these days of non-literacy, it is always helpful to be able to give a child a leaflet or booklet that summarises appropriate parts of the Gospel message, and gives them information to which they can respond as the Holy Spirit works in them. However, a glance at what is available in Christian bookshops reveals that the majority seems to be the same as adult literature, with bigger print, fewer words and more pictures. They all seem to follow the same pattern: 'God loves you, but you are a sinner, cut off from God. Unless you repent and believe what Christ has done on the cross, you will not go to heaven!' Of all the samples I have seen (and used over the years), none seems to acknowledge that a child might already have some kind of relationship with God, and that the correct response may be to affirm, perhaps formally, that he/she wants to go on in that friendship with Jesus. Neither have I seen a leaflet or booklet that acknowledges that this may not be the first time a child has responded to God and encourages a child in that new response. I know that one major Christian publisher did some fresh work on such a project, but came to the conclusion that more than one booklet was necessary, which, I gather, was too big a financial commitment!

Because of this state of affairs, and because I needed literature with which I felt comfortable and confident in its content, a few years ago I wrote my own evangelistic leaflet and booklet, together with one for the child who made another step to Jesus.

These are home-produced to keep costs right down. They may not be perfect, and the writing of this book may encourage me to make some needed improvements, but I am pleased that they have been so useful to so many who work with children.[8]

I am also aware in these days of non-literacy, when children do not read books but are constantly watching a television, that we ask a lot of children when we expect them to read a booklet – and, of course, the Bible. There have been cartoon versions of evangelistic booklets, even of the Bible itself, but these may still represent a huge barrier to many. Of course, I am convinced that the best use of literature is to follow up personal conversation or teaching, rather than 'off-the-shelf' reading. Although there are problems of cost, I believe there is enormous scope for the video or audio 'booklet'. As I write, I am aware of developments in cassette recordings of Bible reading notes, and even of a children's video version of the famous *Journey into Life* evangelistic booklet by Norman Warren. [9]

A third consequence is about the sort of evangelism that is appropriate to children. On this most recent writers are united: it is teaching-evangelism or evangelistic teaching which is the appropriate way, to enable children to come back to God as and when they stray, and to keep going on the journey. Children cannot respond to a God they do not know, or even know about. This is despite the stories that are beginning to be reported of Jesus revealing Himself in visions to children of other faiths and none. Some of these accounts indicate that without any prior information, the children know it is Jesus and that He is the Son of God. This seems to be a fulfilment of the contemporary prophecy of Jean Darnall reported in detail earlier in this book. Such revelation must be considered as the exception, rather than the rule, and the Church must double its efforts to tell the Bible story in ways that are attractive and effective. Along with *the* story must go contemporary stories – accounts of God's dealings with people since Bible times, describing some of the events that have made us what we are. I also believe that just as Jesus spoke of the Kingdom and demonstrated some of its works, so we, too, must be prepared to give the message, 'not with wise and persuasive words, but with a demonstration of the Spirit's power, so that ... faith might not rest on men's wisdom, but on God's power' (1 Cor. 2:4,5). We must by all means show that our God is the living God, and not merely an ideology or 'fairy tale' that normal people grow out of when they are older.

Practically, I feel this means that we must be very careful

not to manipulate or bribe children into the Kingdom. My own preference would be to let such 'demonstrations of the Spirit's power' be effected by other children, rather than adults. Indeed, this is what is beginning to happen in greater measure, as children naturally express the supernatural. I am thrilled with the stories of children praying over their friends for healing in the school playground, often resulting in those friends wanting to know more about Jesus. As long as these things are signposts, and truly point to Jesus and the Kingdom of heaven, I am more than happy. One great problem, it seems, may arise because Western society still views the supernatural as the province of the occult. Non-Christians may rightly be concerned to see children doing supernatural things. Playing with a Ouija board may be considered 'harmless'(!), but they may not be so happy about children exhibiting the biblical supernatural. We have yet to see what will transpire.

One of my 'hard questions' concerned the context of the family. There has been a growing trend that sees evangelism among children as only being truly effective when it occurs within the context of the family. 'If we get the parents, we'll get the children,' is one line of thinking. Others are more concerned that if we do not share the good news of Jesus with children in the context of their family, 'We are in danger of undermining the role of parents and even placing the child under undue pressures'.[10] However, if we pour all our resources into that style of evangelism, there are thousands of children in this country who will never really be given the chance to hear and receive the good news about Jesus! If we feel we cannot reach out to children without the parents, then we may be denying the fact that some of those children will be the first – and possibly the last – in their families to turn to Christ. This is not to deny the fact that children have the best chance of nurture and growth if the parents also come to Christ. The plea is not to neglect those other children.

I have not given attention to evangelistic methods and strategies for reaching out to children who are as yet outside the Church. Others have written especially on those themes.

What most influenced you for Christ as a child? If you consciously came to faith as an adult, what prevented you from hearing about, and responding to, Jesus when you were a child?

Which model of faith in children described in this chapter is most helpful to you?
In what way does it affect your work with children?

Try and write an evangelistic leaflet that would help children you know to respond to God's love in Jesus. What age-range would it suit?

8

Gifts to make us useful to God

The gifts of the Holy Spirit are tools to enable us to do the works of the Kingdom – the things God wants us to do as disciples. It is wise to note that St John, in his Gospel, called the miracles of Jesus 'signs', for that is what they were and still are. They point to the rule or Kingdom of God. For instance, healing miracles point to the time when 'there will be no more death or mourning or crying or pain . . .' (Rev. 21:4), and miracles over the natural world order serve to point us to the time when 'the creation itself will be liberated from its bondage to decay and brought into the glorious freedom of the children of God' (Rom. 8:20).

There are other words that help us to understand the nature of these gifts from God. For instance St Paul, in 1 Corinthians 12:4–6 uses the word 'gift' (*charismata*) and two other words – 'ministries' (*diakoniai*) and 'working' (*energemata*). Each word teaches us essential things about this ministry of God the Holy Spirit. 'Gift' or 'present' is a word that has *charis* as its stem. This is the word for God's grace, His undeserved favour. God offers His gifts freely, with 'no strings attached', just as He offers His unconditional love for us in Christ. 'Ministries' or 'service' is formed from two Greek words, which literally mean 'eager readiness to serve'. The third word, 'working' or 'outworking' reminds us that these gifts produce definite effects, for the strengthening of the Church, for helping the individual, and for the glory of God. St Paul then goes on to say that they are 'the manifestation of the Spirit' (1 Cor. 12:7). Just as the fruits of the Spirit are manifestations of the character of Jesus being formed in us through our life in the Holy Spirit, so the gifts are another manifestation of our usefulness and availability to the Spirit for service.

How can this help children who have experienced the power of the Holy Spirit? It can help because we teach them right from the start that these gifts are not trophies to be kept in a glass cupboard. It can help because we can continue to remind the children that God gives these things out of love for us and His Church, and because He wants us to be useful to Him in bringing about His purposes in the world. We are 'saved to serve', following the example of Jesus.

It is important to note that there are 'different kinds of gifts' (1 Cor. 12:4). The list in this letter of St Paul is just one. The Bible mentions many other gifts and ministries, e.g. Romans 12:4–8 and Ephesians 4:11–13. Christian scholars have different interpretations about God's gifts. From these three New Testament lists some argue that there is a difference between gifts from God, gifts from Christ and gifts from the Holy Spirit. Some of the gifts are more dramatic than the others, and it is easy to give them more attention. For this reason St Paul draws the analogy of the body, in which all parts are essential for the efficient functioning of a human being.

From my understanding and interpretation of what the Bible says, I believe that God wants to use every Christian – 'to each one is given the manifestation of the Spirit . . .' (1 Cor. 12:7), 'Each one should use whatever gift he [she] has received to serve others . . .' (1 Pet. 4:10). We cannot choose which gift or manifestation we should have, but we can ask God for what we need at a given moment. At other times it is God who takes the initiative and prompts us to act in faith. Then we have a choice to use the gift – to obey the prompting of the Holy Spirit and step out in faith to glorify God – or not to use it, for we can 'quench the Spirit'. Many teachers interpret the Bible as teaching that we have *a* gift, and that in some way it becomes our possession. However, it seems from experience and from Scripture that the Spirit can manifest Himself through us in different ways. We may be used in evangelism, in prophecy, in healing and in administration, each time under the prompting and power of the same Holy Spirit. We may find ourselves being used in one particular way more often than others, and thus, when this is recognised by our local church, we may receive that as a ministry. The danger, of course, is that we become inflexible, and refuse to acknowledge that God may want to use us in a different way at some time. This may happen as he challenges our willingness to 'trust and obey'. What might have happened if Ananias had responded to his vision by saying, '. . . but I don't do healing. My gift is preaching, and this guy Saul is not so fond of Christian preachers. I think I must be imagining this rather fanciful picture I'm getting . . .'? We don't know if Ananias had been used in any similar way before. All we know is that he trusted and obeyed, and the result was the ministry of the apostle Paul (Acts 10:10–19).

Another aspect of this gifting from God concerns what might be called 'natural gifts'. In the Old Testament there are other gifts and skills that are God-given that would seem to fall into this category.

Then the Lord said to Moses, 'See I have chosen Bezalel son of Uri, the son of Hur, of the tribe of Judah, and I have filled him with the Spirit of God, with skill, ability and knowledge in all kinds of crafts – to make artistic designs for work in gold, silver and bronze, to cut and set stones, to work in wood, and to engage in all kinds of craftsmanship. Moreover, I have appointed Oholiab son of Ahisamach, of the tribe of Dan, to help him. Also I have given skill to all the craftsmen to make everything I have commanded you: the Tent of Meeting, the ark of the Testimony with the atonement cover on it, and all the other furnishings of the tent . . .' (Exod. 31:1–7).

We cannot say that such 'natural gifts' are in any way lesser gifts. The gift of craftsmanship is clearly a gift from God. David's skill in music (1 Sam. 16:18,23) is another example. The question then follows – are all natural talents gifts from God? Of course, in one sense the answer is yes, but it does not necessarily make it a gift or manifestation of the Holy Spirit. Some of these God-given abilities can be and are used to do anything but glorify God and fulfil His purposes. I was helped by the late Revd David Watson, who once said that 'any gift or talent can be truly a gift of the Holy Spirit when it is used at God's inspiration, in God's power, for God's glory'. Those three conditions are the real test of the nature of a gift.

It may be worth saying here that some see psychic gifts in the same way, as a 'natural gift' that can be used for good or evil. Whether or not this is true, I do know that many have surrendered these abilities to God on conversion, and found that they never have those abilities again. The psychic world is also a fallen world. It is 'occult' because it is hidden and is dangerous for us. This issue may not occur with the children with whom we work, but it is as well to have given it some thought.

The more important point is that some children will have natural talents, and that we begin to train them to surrender those gifts to the Lordship of Christ, and to begin to use them under the three conditions mentioned above. In addition, each child may be anointed with one or other of the supernatural gifts of the Holy Spirit on different occasions. Many people think that if it is supernatural, then it is something to do with the occult – evil power. That is not true, of course. The devil has stolen and twisted God's good gifts and made false or counterfeit ones. No one would make a false or counterfeit £3 note, because there is no such genuine thing. The devil makes false demonstrations of supernatural power to deceive people and lead them away from God. The true and real supernatural power of the Holy Spirit points to the Lord Jesus and to God the Father.

St Paul urges us to 'eagerly desire spiritual gifts, especially the gift of prophecy . . . I would like every one of you to speak in tongues, but I would rather have you prophesy . . . try to excel in gifts that build up the church . . .' (1 Cor. 14:1,5,12). Some children will find themselves manifesting one particular gift with special effect quite often. This may be recognised as the beginnings of a ministry. Such discernment as to whether God is setting a child apart for a particular work is part of the role of leadership. St Paul wrote to Timothy, his 'true son in the faith', '. . . to fan into flame the gift of God, which is in you through the laying on of my hands' (2 Tim. 1:6). We might conclude that as we begin to recognise a particular gifting in a child, we might begin to pray with the laying-on of hands for the increase of that gift 'in proportion to his [her] faith' (Rom. 12:6). It is as well to remember that it has been reckoned that 80 per cent of those called to be missionaries received their 'call' as children and young people. Is it not reasonable to suppose that the same may be true of other ministries?

God uses kids!

This book began with the reminder that God has always used children, as well as grown-ups, to do His work. God uses

kids. Discipleship begins as soon as we begin to follow Jesus, not just when we are adults. God wants to equip every Christian for the tasks He has planned for us, so that God's family, the Church, can be all that God wants it to be (Eph. 4:1 1–16). When a child has begun to experience God's power, then is the time to use it – to be useful to Father God.

I believe there are four 'keys' to being useful to God.

Availability. God will use us if we are not too busy for Him to speak to us and tell us when He wants to use us. We get better at this when we spend time regularly talking to Him in prayer, and reading His Word, the Bible. Jesus was the Son of God, but still He had to make time to be alone with God (e.g. Luke 5:16). He said, '. . . I do nothing on my own but speak just what the Father has taught me' (John 8:28).

Willingness. God will use us if we want Him to! He never makes us do anything we don't want to do. Someone has said that God commands but does not compel. We have the freedom of choice to obey or not to obey. A man with a dreaded skin disease said to Jesus, 'Lord, if you are willing, you can make me clean' (Matt. 8:2). We need to be willing, because of the consequences. The disciples often found themselves in trouble for being willing to be used by God. We need to be prepared for whatever may come as a result of our willingness.

Flexibility. This means we are willing to do whatever God wants, even if it is something new or different. When there is a need, God will often use the first available, willing and flexible person He can find! Stephen was 'a man full of God's grace and power' and 'did great wonders and miraculous signs among the people . . .' (Acts 6:8). It was because he was 'full of faith and of the Holy Spirit' (6:5) that he was chosen, not to be a great preacher or healer or prophet, but 'to wait on tables' (6:2). Stephen was flexible, but I believe that his willingness to be used by God in any way, no matter how humble, led to his powerful ministry – and to his martyrdom.

Faith. If we want to be useful to God, we must believe that God really does want to use us, even if we are children. We need to be aware that children are often assailed with doubts, and that they need constant reassurance and faith-building ministry. Not only is the 'father of lies', the devil, feeding their minds, but even well-meaning adults often crush them, saying they are too young, or not good enough. Remember, even the disciples got it wrong about children (Mark 10: 13,14). If a child really loves Jesus, and that is why they want to be useful to God, we can believe what God says – He wants to use them.

Tongues – a gift for all God's children

'The one who speaks in ... tongues helps [edifies, builds up] only himself...' (1 Cor. 14:4 GN). The Revd David Watson used to call tongues 'God's personal baptism gift', for although there are many gifts of the Holy Spirit, this is the only one for which one use is just for our personal help and growth in our love for Jesus.

Perhaps it is for this reason that the gift of tongues is the only one from the 'supernatural list' that Jesus did not use. Some have concluded that it is in some way inferior or suspect, but I find no scriptural warrant for that attitude. It is a gift that causes no small controversy, either because of the classical Pentecostal view that it is the only evidence of a true experience of the Spirit (with which I disagree), or because of the difficulty so many people have in doing it! One interesting thing is that it appears that some children have used this gift in their prayer life since infancy without knowing it! Lest any sceptic will point out that most small children talk 'scribble', those who make this claim about the infant experience say that the children concerned are aware of the difference between the two.

This is not the place to justify the gift of tongues, and most readers, I suspect, need no such persuasion. However, some may want to be convinced about the appropriateness of the gift for children. There is no specific biblical evidence of children speaking in tongues, but neither is there such evidence for a child leading someone to Christ! One cannot argue either way from silence. I have also felt that one purpose of the gift is to enable Christians to learn to step out in faith, doing something that relies entirely on God (except for the use of our voice). From a logical point of view, I think it is wonderful that children, who generally have a more limited vocabulary, are enabled through the Holy Spirit to pray in

113

words that are exactly right, for they are inspired by the co-operation of the Holy Spirit and the human spirit. Some might be alarmed at the thought of children going home from the children's group and saying to (possibly) non-Christian parents, 'Look what I can do!' and proceeding to speak in tongues! It is often difficult enough when a child goes home and announces, 'I'm a Christian, now!' If God releases this gift in a child spontaneously, then that is His 'problem', as it were, but if we plan to teach and offer to pray with a child to receive the gift as part of the general policy to see children equipped for Christian discipleship, then parents do need to be warned, as has been discussed in an earlier chapter.

How, then, can we teach about the gift, and enable a child to receive it? First, we can teach that this is one of the ways God helps us to praise and worship Him.

Help to praise and worship God.   Jesus said, 'God is Spirit, and only by the power of his Spirit can people worship him as he really is' (John 4:24 GN). Whenever we want to worship God, we should ask the Holy Spirit to help us. How will He do this? Jesus said the Holy Spirit will 'teach you all things and will remind you of everything I have said to you' (John 14:26). When we remember what God has done and how good He is, we want to thank Him and give Him our praise. Praise is very important. We can ask if the children remember the disappointment of Jesus when He healed the ten men who had the skin disease. He was disappointed because only one came back to say 'Thanks', even though all of them were healed.

We can explain that there is one supernatural gift that God gives which is specially to help us to praise God, explaining that 'supernatural' means that it is not natural – it is not something we're born with – it is something God gives, and the gift of course is 'tongues'. It is important to explain that the word in the Bible can also mean 'languages', because that is what the gift is about. Without anyone sitting down to learn it, God the Holy Spirit gives the ability to speak out God's praise in another language. We can't choose the language, and we may never know what it is. The Bible seems to indicate that the language might be an earthly one – or even a language used by angels! (See 1 Corinthians 13:1.)

On a personal note, there was an occasion when I was on a mission team from Anglican Renewal Ministries. We had been explaining the place of spiritual gifts in the Church, and one elderly clergyman asked if we might demonstrate some of these gifts during the Eucharist that was to follow. The archdeacon agreed, and so we asked God to 'do His stuff'. To my surprise and pleasure, a short while later I felt God's prompting to speak aloud in tongues, something which I had not done for some months. I stood and spoke out, hoping that I was right, and probably hoping to impress the clergyman concerned! Another person stood and interpreted what I had said. It was good and positive, but nothing earth-shattering. However, after the service another cleric approached me and said that he and his family had been missionaries in southern Africa, and did I know that I had spoken in a near perfect Bantu dialect? I had to admit that I did not even know what Bantu was. He further added that the interpretation that was given was also correct, even though that person knew nothing of this language! One hears of this kind of story in other countries, etc., but this happened to me! It is not a 'proof' about tongues, but it throws light on the mysterious nature of the variety of languages God may choose to dispense in this gift.

Praising tongues.   When we are praising God and find it hard to say all that we feel about God in our worship, it is as if God the Holy Spirit helps us to express that praise in words which He provides! This means that although we might not know what we are saying because we haven't learnt to understand the language, we know that we are giving God real praise from our hearts. St Paul says, 'anyone who speaks in a tongue does not speak to men but to God ... no-one understands him; he utters mysteries with his spirit' (1 Cor. 14:2). The Holy Spirit sometimes tells us what we are saying, too.

Praying tongues. At other times, we need the Spirit's help in asking God for something. When we are praying for someone or some situation and we don't know how to pray, we can use this 'praise and prayer language'. (See Romans 8:26.)

In the tradition of many teachers, I often use stories to teach, stories based on real incidents. Here is the kind of story I tell to introduce this particular gift:

Tom came home from the 'Kids' Praise' very excited. 'Emma, it was great! You should have come! I got the gift of tongues!'

'What do you mean? What's tongues?' asked Emma, rather crossly.

'Well, it's a kind of funny language that God helps you speak when He fills you with the Holy Spirit. Listen ...' Tom began to make some very funny sort of sounds, a bit like a foreign language.

Emma laughed because of the funny face Tom was making as he made the sounds. 'You're making it up!' she laughed.

'I'm not, honest,' said Tom, annoyed that Emma wasn't a little bit envious. 'The bloke at the Kids' Praise prayed with those who wanted to receive tongues. He said that after he'd prayed we should start to praise God – tell Him how much we thought of Him, and how glad we are that He really loves us and stuff like that. Then he said we should stop speaking in English, and just speak out the sounds that come to our mind.'

'And you got those funny sounds?' said Emma, still not sure about this 'tongues' thing that was exciting her brother so much.

'Yeah. I wasn't sure if I was making it up, really, but the man said that if we thought we were making it up, we should just ask God to accept the sounds as something we really want to give to Him. He said that it was unlikely we were making it up anyway! Anyway, I know it wasn't me doing it – it was the Holy Spirit in me.'

'Was the Holy Spirit making you speak tongues – like a ventri- ventrol- – one of those people with a puppet that talks?' asked Emma, a bit more interested.

'No – 'cos sometimes I stopped just to see what others were doing. Anyway, the man said that just like the disciples in the Bible we have to give God our voice – we do the speaking, but the Holy Spirit makes the words.'

'They don't sound like real words,' said Emma, trying to copy the sounds Tom had made earlier.

'The man said that it might be one of thousands of languages from around the world – or even a language that angels speak!'

'Gosh!' said Emma. 'Can I do it, too?' She began to make some gurgling sounds, but they both laughed at the result!

'I think we ought to ask Glen,' said Tom, meaning the leader of their kids' group at church. 'I've still got questions I want to ask, and you can find out if you can get the gift of tongues, too!'

Please note, many children have never heard speaking in tongues. The very term may give them all kinds of strange ideas in their imagination (remember that junior-age children are concrete thinkers). It may be helpful for you to use your gift of tongues (if you have it) out loud simply in order for them to hear what it is like. Explain that this is not usually how you use the gift, and that you may not understand what you mean. This may result in some giggles as they hear you speak, but it may put worried minds at rest, especially as they see you are not in some kind of trance, shouting or doing anything else strange.

You may feel that this is enough at first, and may wish to proceed to pray for the children to receive the gift. However, I feel it is also important to teach that there are other uses of the gift of tongues in the Bible, whether or not you wish to go into detail at this stage.

First, the experience of the disciples on the day of Pentecost was that although they did not understand what they were saying, those who heard them *did* understand, for they were speaking in their language: '. . . we hear them declaring the wonders of God in our own tongues!' (Acts 2:11). Although there are reports of this happening since that time, it is not common.

However, the other use of tongues is in public worship, when it is followed by an interpretation, also inspired by the Holy Spirit. St Paul writes, 'I would like all of you to speak in . . . tongues, but I would rather that you had the gift of proclaiming God's message [prophecy] . . . unless there is someone present who can explain what he says . . .' (1 Cor. 14:5 GN). Many people feel a special urge to speak out loud in tongues. This is often a different kind of gift of tongues to the one we have as a private prayer and praise language. When this happens, and it really is a God-given urge, He will always give another gift, so that everyone can know what it means. This is the interpretation of tongues (see 1 Cor. 12:10). God often gives the gift of interpretation to someone else in the meeting, but St Paul says that whoever 'speaks in a tongue should pray that he may interpret what he [she] says' (1 Cor. 14:13). The interpretation may be a 'message' from God to those who are gathered together, but many Christians believe it is always words spoken *to* God.

Here is another episode of the story I use to teach these things:

Tom and Emma had received the gift of tongues – the 'praise and prayer' language from the Holy Spirit – some weeks ago. Tom had showed off his new ability like a toy he'd got for Christmas. 'God's given me a special gift – listen . . .' he'd said to others in the Wayfinders group at church. Some had laughed at the sounds he made, others had been worried and some were jealous. Glen, their leader, had to do a lot of sorting out, explaining and teaching what the Bible said about this gift from God.

Emma felt quite embarrassed about it all. Emma was a year older than nine-year-old Tom. She loved Jesus and the special times she had being quiet with God meant a lot to her. She told Him everything and knew He understood everything in a way no one else did. It was in those times that she used her praise and prayer language and she knew it was saying something very important from deep inside. It had horrified her when Tom had spoken out loud in tongues at Wayfinders, and she thought he'd done something very wrong indeed.

Glen had sorted things out, and explained things very carefully, but Emma was still very embarrassed at what she was now feeling. It was a special Wayfinder prayer meeting. There had been some singing, and it felt as if God was especially close to them all. Had she been by herself, Emma would have been quietly talking away to God in her praise language. But she was with eight others as well as Tom and Glen.

She felt she was going to burst – she had to say something, but didn't know what, except that it was going to be
in tongues! Nearly in tears, she quietly asked God to help
her. Then, taking a deep breath, she began to speak.

It didn't take long, but to Emma it felt like hours! She felt
so relieved when at last she stopped – she didn't dare open
her eyes as she felt everyone in the room was looking at
her.

Quietly, in a matter-of-fact way, Glen asked if anyone felt
they knew what Emma had said.

'How could they?' thought Emma, 'It's my tongue, no
one knows what I'm thinking!'

Then Tom began to speak. 'It's like I know what Emma
was saying – not what the words mean, but what she was
saying.'

'Tell us, Tom,' said Glen, gently. Tom did so, in only a
few words.

Emma thought he hadn't said it all, but knew at the same
time that he was right – it sort of felt right inside.

'Thank you, Tom, and thank you, Emma,' said Glen. 'I
think that was the Holy Spirit teaching you another way in
which He uses the gift of tongues, Emma. And you, Tom,
had what the Bible calls the gift of interpretation.'

How can children actually receive the gift? Although there
are many cases of children receiving it spontaneously, the
usual way is to ask in prayer. Sometimes the teaching is given
as part of the preparation for receiving the empowering of the
Holy Spirit, but that is not necessary, and can be a different
occasion. My own practice is to let the children have a
'confession time', to make sure there is nothing stopping the
flow of the Holy Spirit. Then I pray, asking the Holy Spirit to
come near, and for Father God to give His good gifts to those
who sincerely ask Him. Then, as with the infilling of the

Spirit, I invite the children to ask for the gift themselves, out loud, when they are ready. Meanwhile I will continue to pray for them in tongues, sometimes also singing in tongues quietly. Some actually suggest that the children attempt to imitate the tongues they are hearing, realising that what the children will actually do is to speak in their own tongue.

The other major question asked by most people at this time is, 'What if I am making it up?' My reply is that if I really want to worship Jesus, then even if I am making it up, Jesus will not reject what I give Him. A four-year-old child may take only a few seconds to draw a picture which she gives to me. It is clearly not thought out, or done carefully, yet I will never reject and deride it. It is still given as a gift. If I can graciously accept such an offering, how much more will Jesus receive what we offer Him sincerely. The main thing is that we cross the sound barrier – our own voice making sounds that seem strange to our ears. I venture to suggest that even if we start by making it up, the Holy Spirit soon takes over, and it is His words we are speaking. Some children receive the gift with great emotion, but others do not. I teach that children should practise their gift for at least five minutes each day, either speaking or singing.

Occasionally, someone just cannot break the sound barrier. I generally advise them to think of a worship song they love to sing to Jesus. I suggest they go away where no one can hear them, and sing the song out loud two or three times, and then, having asked the Holy Spirit to help them, I suggest they sing it out loud again, this time singing words or sounds that just come to their mind. Again, I suggest they simply offer it to Jesus as the best they have to offer at the moment. Many have found this to be the key to unlocking this basic gift of God the Holy Spirit.

While St Paul says, 'I thank God that I speak in tongues more than all of you' (1 Cor. 14:18), he urges us to 'eagerly desire spiritual gifts, especially the gift of prophecy' (1 Cor. 14:1). Thus we move on to examine how that and the other supernatural gifts can be manifested in and through children, whether or not they have spoken in tongues.

9

Prophecy and other gifts of the Holy Spirit in and through children

The gifts set out in St Paul's letter to the Corinthians are a list of supernatural manifestations of the Holy Spirit. They are supernaturally given, and are not inborn traits. I believe it is these supernatural manifestations that enable children to minister to adults in a special way, because they are not dependent on knowledge, skill or maturity – though the effectiveness of each can be increased with knowledge, skill and maturity! The key quality for ministering in these gifts, however, is faith, and that is why the ministry of children is often so powerful. The faith of a child has a special quality, a purity that probably diminishes as a child gets older and learns adult rational thought processes which can clash with simple faith. Although children can and do minister to adults, I feel it is more usual for them to minister primarily to other children. This is safer, and less controversial, though I believe we are learning more about these things as time goes on.

Prophecy

I normally introduce this topic in the same way I introduce the 'pictures experiment' mentioned in an earlier chapter.

God wants to speak to His creation, His children. God has 'spoken' to us – given us His most important 'message' – when He sent Jesus (Heb. 1:1,2). Jesus is God's great 'message' that He loves us and has a plan for our lives, that we may be forgiven for our sins and receive a new life by faith in Jesus, that we may receive the Holy Spirit in our lives, making us the people we were meant to be.

The Bible itself is God's 'Word' to us. Christians believe it is the measure by which to judge if something is true or false. If someone has a 'message' from God now, the first test to see if it is true is to see if it goes against what the Bible says.

In the Old Testament part of the Bible we read of men (and sometimes women) who were called prophets. These were mighty people of God, called to live lives fully surrendered to God, given messages to speak that were not welcomed by those who were meant to receive them. Sometimes their messages foretold the future, because God was warning people what would happen if they did not change their wicked ways.

In the New Testament part of the Bible, we read of another gift of prophecy (1 Cor. 14:1, 5), but this time it is not just for a special few. God still wants to speak to us. Sometimes it may be about the future (a warning or a promise), but it is often words of encouragement for us to keep growing in our love for God, or some kind of instruction as to what God wants us to do. As with Jeremiah (Jer. 1:11–14) and Amos (Amos 7:1,2; 8:1,2), pictures are just one way in which God speaks His message, and often a good way of starting to speak out what we think God is saying. This gift, like all the others, has to be learnt. We do not get it perfectly right at first – or indeed, ever (see 1 Cor. 13:9) – but God still wants to use us in this way. In my reference to the gift of pictures, I have already hinted that it is a short step from this, at a time when the children are quiet, to invite the Spirit of Jesus to speak some words into our hearts that He wants to say to someone else.

Here is the story I use as an illustration:

Chloe was in the Christian Union at school. They met every Tuesday lunchtime in Room 14b. Over the past few weeks Miss Williamson had been teaching them about ways God wants to speak through Christians.

'You must be a very holy person to get a message from God,' thought Chloe, 'someone like Susan.' Susan was a vicar's daughter. She knew her Bible back to front, it seemed. She was always quoting it.

'It must be wonderful to have a faith like Susan's. I wish I could be like her,' Chloe had often thought.

Today, Miss Williamson had been very quick, and there were fifteen minutes before the bell would go for the afternoon lessons. Amanda played her guitar as they sang a worship song. Then Miss Williamson had suggested they be quiet and listen to see if God wanted to speak to them now.

Chloe felt sure if God was going to speak through anyone, it would be Susan, but Susan was just very quiet. Then Chloe suddenly realised she was not really listening to God, and tried to be quiet inside herself.

To her surprise she suddenly felt herself thinking these words: 'Don't be afraid, I will be with you.'

'I'm not afraid,' thought Chloe to herself. 'What a silly thought.'

Then Miss Williamson spoke up quietly. 'I think God has given someone here a message – a prophecy. Will whoever it is speak it out?'

Chloe looked around to see who had got the message from God – was it Susan? But Susan still had her head down in prayer.

'Has anyone got any words in their mind?' asked Miss Williamson.

Chloe spoke up. 'All I've got, Miss, is these words: don't be afraid, I will be with you ... but it's not really a prophecy, Miss ...'

But then Susan began to cry. It seemed that Susan's father was going to become vicar of another church many miles away. Susan was so scared of moving away, leaving her friends. When Chloe had said those eight words, it felt as though God was speaking directly to her. It was still hard to move, but Susan believed God really was with her and would help her find new friends.

Chloe could hardly believe that God had spoken through her – had given her a gift of prophecy for that meeting.

Some people are very cautious about the idea of getting it wrong, and putting their own words into God's mouth ('Thus saith the Lord ...' etc.). It seems no problem to me to precede the message with words such as, 'I feel the Lord is saying something like this ...' However, having introduced the message, I always train the one giving the prophecy to speak as a biblical messenger would speak, i.e. in the first person. For instance, no messenger in those times would come and say, 'The King is very pleased with you, and he wants to show you his pleasure. In three days' time he will visit you and invite you to spend time with him ...' A true messenger simply passes on the message as he heard it, for in this way he is not interpreting it. The correct way of passing on that message would be, 'The King says, "I am very pleased with you, and I want to show my pleasure. In three days I will visit you, and I want you to come and spend time with me ..."'

This is a very powerful ministry, and for this reason many people are cautious about it. I have known cases of self-appointed prophets saying what God is going to do, but it never happens. The disappointment and hurt inflicted can be considerable. Should this make us wary of exercising the gift, or encouraging children to prophesy? I would say that children are not generally manipulators – it is adults who tend to manipulate children. There are three sources of revelation: the human spirit, the Holy Spirit and unclean spirits. It is no surprise that closely linked with this gift in St Paul's list is the gift of discernment of spirits.

Discerning of spirits

Many Christians have largely forgotten this link, but many scholars agree that its prime purpose is to monitor prophetic words. This is understandable if the New Testament expectation was that everyone would prophesy. How could the genuine be sorted out from the false?

St Paul talks a lot about the 'sinful nature', especially in his letters to Christians in Rome (Rom. 7,8). When we begin to follow Jesus, we become 'a brand-new person inside' (2 Cor. 5:17 LB). But we often find ourselves trying to do what the old part of us wants, the part of us that still wants to put 'me first' before God, what the Bible calls 'the old nature'. Because of Jesus, and His death on the cross, 'we can obey God's laws if we follow after the Holy Spirit and no longer obey the old evil nature within us' (Rom. 8:4 LB). But we still have a battle, and we need God's help. That is another part of the work of the Holy Spirit, day by day making us more like Jesus in the kind of person He was.

Sometimes people say and do things which seem good, but really they are only showing off, or pretending to do what God wants when it is really just what they want.

In the 'KJB' ('Know Jesus Better') group, they had been having some really good meetings, with the Holy Spirit giving words and pictures to different members of the group. Tim had shared some words which he thought God had given to him in his mind, and it was very helpful to a lot of people.

The following week, Tim shared some more words which he said God had given him. They sounded good, and all the people in the group nodded their heads in agreement, all, that is, except Anna and Mike, the group leader.

'Mike,' Anna whispered, 'I don't think that was really from God. It sounds all right, but something inside me makes me feel it wasn't.'

'I know what you mean, Anna,' whispered Mike in reply, 'I think the Holy Spirit is giving what the Bible calls the gift of discernment.'

Anna didn't know what that was, as they hadn't talked about that gift yet, but she was pleased that Mike thought she was right. After the meeting, Mike had a quiet talk with Tim, explaining what he felt God had showed Anna and himself. Tim was angry at first, but then went very red and tearful.

'It felt so good giving that prophecy last week. Everyone thought I was really good. I suppose I wanted people to think the same this week, too,' Tim said. 'I'm sorry, Mike. Was it very bad?'

'No, it wasn' bad, Tim, just daft! We like you for who you are, not for pretending to be someone you're not – not yet, anyway!' said Mike. 'There's no need to say anything to the group unless you want to. You might like to say sorry to God, though, before the devil convinces you you've done something really bad! At least it's reminded me to explain about this gift of discernment to the group, though!'

At these times, it is not an evil spirit that is making someone do things like this, but the 'old nature' – the human spirit.

This is why I believe that this way in which God's power works through the Christian is so important, especially for the young follower, because they do not have the natural wisdom or maturity to know what lies behind the words and actions that are said and done around us. The gift of discernment most often shows us something that is good – that a picture or prophecy really is from God, and should be listened to (even if it's not absolutely perfect!). This gift is not just about recognising evil or wrong things.

However, we do need to explain about the enemies against whom we fight as followers of Jesus. In the story about Tim, the source of his 'prophecy' was his own human spirit. The Bible also teaches us about an enemy called Satan or the devil. I simply explain that it seems he was an angel who was thrown out of heaven because he wanted to be like God Himself (Isa. 14:12–15; Luke 10:18). This enemy has taken over the world like an invading army, spoiling it and everything in it (see John 14:30). Satan is God's enemy, but he is ours if we are trying to live God's way. Thus the Bible says, 'Your enemy the devil prowls around like a roaring lion looking for someone to devour' (1 Pet. 5:8).

God's enemy the devil wants to trap or deceive us, leading us away from what God says is true and right, as he tried to do with Jesus when He was tempted in the wilderness (Luke 4:1–13). Sometimes he uses people, by the things they say and do – even when they seem so good. At these times their words and actions are inspired by evil spirits (which I explain as angelic beings that do the devil's work). A biblical example of this can be found where Paul and Silas were in Philippi, and a fortune-telling slave girl followed them about, shouting, 'These men are servants of the Most High God, who are telling you the way to be saved' (Acts 16:17). She was right, but still, 'Paul became so troubled that he turned round and said to the spirit, "In the name of Jesus Christ I command you to come out of her!" At that moment the spirit left her' (Acts 16:18).

The gift of discernment is valuable – even essential – in this kind of case, too. How we need it in these days of New Age thinking. The following story may help in teaching this aspect:

Jane was taken by her mum to see a faith healer, because she had eczema, a skin disease, that no doctors seemed able to cure. The healer was a nice man who used a thing on a string as he said some words over Jane. Jane and her mum were really thrilled when Jane's skin began immediately to get better, but Jane soon began to have really frightening dreams.

At school, she talked with her friend Alison who went to the school Christian Union, wondering if she would pray for her.

'When did you start having the bad dreams, Jane?' she asked.

'Not long after I was cured of my eczema,' explained Jane, telling her friend about the faith healer.

Something made Alison unhappy about the faith healer, and she talked with the teacher in charge of the school Christian Union, Miss Williamson. The teacher arranged to visit Jane and her mum at home.

When she came, she explained about healers whose power came from the devil, even though they thought it was from God.

'I think the man's power was not from God, Mrs Taylor. The Bible teaches us that to seek healing from such people is wrong and we must confess it to God. If you do that, I'll pray with you and ask the Lord Jesus to bring His good healing. If I'm wrong, then no harm will be done.'

Mrs Taylor listened to the teacher and agreed to do as

she suggested. Jane and her mum asked for God's forgiveness if they had done anything wrong, and Miss Williamson prayed for Jane. Within days, the bad dreams had stopped, and at first the eczema began to return. But that, too, began to improve as Alison and other Christian friends began to pray for Jane.

That 'something that made her unhappy' Alison had felt was God giving her the gift of discernment about the healer and the cause of Jane's bad dreams. This is a further manifestation of the work of the Holy Spirit.

Generally speaking, I feel that the gift of discernment is a leadership gift – a pastor's gift to monitor prophetic words. However, because we are engaged in spiritual warfare, as we keep close to Jesus, the Spirit of Jesus will give us that sensitivity, often without us realising it.

Word of knowledge

This is another 'revelation gift' that is fairly common, but which adults tend to treat as super-rare and special. The thing is that God sometimes tells us things we could never know unless He told us! He won't tell us the answer to questions in exams, though He might remind us about things we have already learnt.

This gift is about more than that, though! When God wants to do something special – for instance to show someone how much He loves them and wants to heal them – He might give a 'word of knowledge'. This comes in many different ways. Some people suddenly feel a pain or ache that is not theirs. God is telling them what someone else is feeling, normally because He wants to heal them in some way. Some people 'see' words, like 'headache' or 'muscle'. As with the other gifts of the Holy Spirit, the only way to 'test' them is to describe them, and see if someone recognises the word or information.

Mrs Rogers was having a cup of coffee with Christopher's mum and dad. When Christopher went into the kitchen for a biscuit, she was holding her head and pulling such a face that he realised she had some kind of headache.

'Mrs Rogers has a migraine, Chris,' said his dad. 'We're just going to pray with her. Would you like to join us?'

Christopher and his family were just beginning to get used to doing things like this together. They had been challenged at a Christian conference to learn to 'minister' together as a family. Christopher was pleased to be included in this special work for God with his mum and dad.

They began to pray. Rather shyly, Christopher asked God to bless Mrs Rogers and heal her. He liked Mrs Rogers a lot, and was concerned about the pain she was having.

All of a sudden, he suddenly got a picture in his mind of a little girl crying. He had heard about having pictures, and so he spoke up.

'Dad, I've just got a picture of a little girl crying. I don't know what it means, though.'

His dad was surprised at his son's words but very pleased.

'That may be God giving us some special information to help us as we pray for Mrs Rogers, Chris,' he said.

Chris's mum spoke to their friend. 'Does that mean anything to you, Vera? Did anything special happen to you as a girl?'

Mrs Rogers was quiet for a bit, then said, 'I'd forgotten about that. There was something . . .' and she began to tell of a time when she had had a terrible shock.

'I think God's telling us that your migraines have got something to do with that shock you had all those years ago,' Chris's dad said. He then prayed about that, asking Jesus to heal the memory of the incident.

The pain went soon after that, and Mrs Rogers never had those migraines again. Chris was amazed that God would give him a 'word of knowledge' – he thought only adults got things like that.

At other times, God tells us something to help us in other ways – it is not always about healing. I love telling children about the amazing word of knowledge that the Holy Spirit gave to Jesus in Matthew 17:24–7. It's the story about Jesus knowing where to get money for the temple tax from a very unusual place! It is the kind of story that foxes some teachers, and many dismiss it as some kind of myth. When we grow accustomed to words of knowledge, however, this is no real surprise to us, even if it is amazing! When we are aware that a child has received a word of knowledge, we should acknowledge it and encourage that child to keep listening for more such revelations at other times.

Word of wisdom

I have already mentioned the example of Jesus receiving a word of wisdom in Jericho, when He looked into the syca-more-fig tree and saw Zacchaeus. The supernatural wisdom was to invite Himself to Zacchaeus' home. There are other examples. For instance, when Jesus was told about the sickness and imminent death of His friend Lazarus, He did not, as any normal friend would, immediately go to Bethany to do something. Instead He stayed where He was. I believe this was because He was obeying His heavenly Father (John 11).

A person may get some information from God, but he or she might not know what to do about it! It was not what Jesus said but what He did that caused Zacchaeus to become a different kind of person. This is the kind of gift of the Holy Spirit that we may receive without knowing it, because we all grow wiser as we grow older. However, it seems that God still needs to give us these bursts of special wisdom, especially when we are doing something that will point to Him in some way. It can also happen to children.

Carl was on holiday with his Uncle Bob and Aunt Sue. They had hired a car and were touring Scotland. One day they travelled to the Isle of Skye, and found a very lonely pebble beach. It was very beautiful and they spent several hours there before they decided to move on.

'Oh no!' his uncle exclaimed.

'What's the matter?' said his aunt.

'I've lost the car keys!'

'Oh no!' said his aunt. 'We're miles from anywhere, where will we get spare keys from?'

'We'd better start searching,' said his uncle, 'but it's like looking for a needle in a haystack!'

Carl realised they could take hours searching and still not find the keys, and then he remembered what he had been learning about 'wisdom' in Junior Church. He had learnt about the 'word of wisdom', and remembered the memory verse he had learnt off by heart.

'Uncle Bob, let's ask God to help us,' he said, and recited the verse: '"If any of you lacks wisdom, he should ask God, who gives generously to all without finding fault, and it will be given to him." James 1:5.'

His uncle gave a smile, and his aunt said, 'I don't think God would be concerned about our carelessness, Carl!'

That didn't stop Carl from turning away and quickly praying in his head, asking for wisdom to know where to look.

Carl thought that there might be a sudden beam of sunlight showing where the keys were, but there was nothing. Then he remembered that when they had arrived at the beach, the tide was in, and they had been walking higher up the beach.

He ran to the tide mark, where there was the usual litter of seaweed and junk washed ashore by the sea. He had taken only a few steps when he saw the bunch of keys! He picked them up and gave a yell of delight!

'I think you're wrong, Auntie Sue, God is concerned to help us, even when we're careless!'

That incident made Carl's aunt and uncle think more about God, though Carl never knew it.

The gifts of faith and miracles

These two gifts are closely linked, though they are not the same. The gift of faith is not the same as the faith God gives us to trust in Jesus for forgiveness and new life as we begin to follow Him.

This special gift of faith is one to help us trust God for something that seems almost impossible and out of the ordinary, as when Jesus said that we could tell a mountain to move and it would (Matt. 17:20)! God might also release this gift of faith as we are praying for someone, which enables them to do something really great.

At the annual Church Holiday Club, it was raining hard – very hard.

Streams of water began to flow through the big tent, and the amplifiers could hardly make the leader's voice heard above the noise of the thunder and the rain hitting the tent roof. The children, especially the little ones, were beginning to be afraid.

135

The band began to play praise songs, with everyone joining in. Then the leader suddenly reminded the children of the time when Jesus had stilled a storm on a lake when He was in a boat.

'Do you believe Jesus did it then?' he asked the children, shouting as loud as he could to be heard.

'Yes!' came the reply, with a surge of faith that could only be God's special gift.

The leader prayed a simple prayer, asking God to stop the storm. The children said a loud 'Amen!', and almost immediately the rain stopped! Within minutes, the Holiday Club programme was running as planned, but everyone knew they had seen a miracle!

The gift of miracles includes healings, but it seems this gift is different, and includes being able to do something that works against the forces of nature, just as when Jesus was able to command the wind to stop blowing and the waves to be still (Mark 4:35–41).

We learn that sometimes we ask God for the miracle because of a situation. However, often we do not recognise this gift as it happens, and only realise what God did when we look back.

Do you remember Tom and Emma's Wayfinders group? One Christmas they decided to have a special party for kids from the travellers' camp. No one liked the travellers, and even church people thought they were not to be trusted. The Wayfinders' leader, Glen, had suggested the idea, and the members of the group thought it would be really good to do something for people who didn't have much, even if it was a bit of a risk.

The travellers were a bit suspicious about it at first, because no one did things like that for nothing as far as they were concerned. Eventually they agreed to let the kids come.

The hall was decorated and food and gifts gathered for about twenty of the traveller children. The kids arrived with a lot of noise and excitement, and the party was a great success.

At the end, when the children had gone home, the Wayfinders set about cleaning and tidying up.

'Glen,' asked Emma, 'where did you get the extra food and presents from?'

'What do you mean?' asked Glen, puzzled.

'Well, you said there were about twenty traveller kids.'

'Yes . . .'

'But there were at least twice that number – you know we had to get extra chairs and tables out for the food.'

'Yes, that's right,' said the leader.

'So where did you get the extra food and presents? I counted everything out beforehand – that was my job. But everyone had plenty to eat, and all those kids went home with a present – I watched them.'

Glen was astonished. He asked Tom and the other Wayfinders, but no one had brought extra food and presents.

'I just gave out the gifts from the black plastic bag without thinking,' said Glen.

'And I just dished out the food on each of the tables,' said Emma.

Everyone went very quiet. Unless some other person, unknown to the group, had provided the extra things, then they had seen – or rather missed – a miracle!

Gift of healing

Of all the special gifts of the Holy Spirit, we probably recognise this one best. We know that Jesus did so much

137

healing, and did it in many different ways. Sometimes He gave a command, like 'Be clean' (Luke 5:13), sometimes He touched the person (Matt. 8:15) and sometimes He gave the sick person a command to obey (Luke 17:14).

Jesus said, 'As the Father sent me, I am sending you' (John 20:21). He sent His disciples to 'preach the kingdom' and to 'heal the sick' (Luke 9:2). It is clear that it is part of our work for Jesus today, and I have already explained the hands-on praying method that I use so much with children (and adults). I believe it is important that we emphasise that doctors and medicine are part of God's healing, as they were in the time Jesus walked on earth. We are to use whatever means God gives to bring about someone's healing.

The other emphasis I make is to remind the children that the Bible talks of people being healed, not cured. Healing is about becoming well or 'whole' in every part of us – our body, our emotions, our mind, our memories and our soul (the part of us that lives on after we die). To become a friend of Jesus and receive new life and the gift of the Holy Spirit is the greatest healing people can receive, but God wants to do more for us.

For example, some men brought their friend to Jesus because he was paralysed. Jesus first of all healed his soul – He forgave the man for the wrong things in his life. It was only then that He healed the man's body (Matt. 9:1–8). It seems that although we might pray for someone's back to be healed, perhaps God might want to heal a bad habit first, because He knows that is more important! It is important to remember this, when the healing does not happen in the way we think or want.

Jamie and Angus were excited because at the Christian camp they went to in the summer, they had seen someone's knee healed through prayer.

Fergus had badly twisted it playing football, and it looked as though he would have to go to hospital. While they were waiting for the ambulance, Andrew had suggested they put their hands on Fergus and ask in the name of Jesus for God's healing power to come on him.

They had never done anything like this before, and they felt a bit embarrassed, but they were amazed as Fergus first of all began to squirm with pain as they prayed, and then began to smile as he felt it going from his knee.

'It's amazing!' he said, 'It hurt like mad, and then I felt it pop back!'

He still went to hospital for a check-up, but he was back soon afterwards – and back on the football pitch the next day!

Back home some weeks later, when their gran became ill, Jamie and Angus went round to her house and asked if they could pray for her.

'Aye,' she said, 'that'd be nice.'

Just as they had done with Fergus, they laid their hands on Gran, and prayed in the name of Jesus for God's healing power to come on the old lady.

Nothing happened.

They prayed some more, using every kind of prayer they could think of, but still nothing seemed to happen.

Tears came to Gran's eyes. 'You're lovely lads,' she said. 'I'm really touched that you came to pray with me.'

But Jamie and Fergus were very disappointed, and realised they had more to learn about healing.

Healing is a mystery. We don't really know why some people are healed and others aren't. My experience is that children can easily cope with this mystery. The point is that when we pray for someone to be healed, we should always be asking God to show us how to pray. As hard as it may seem to us,

God sometimes allows people to die to find their best healing, for after death there is no more pain, no more tears, especially if the person is a Christian and has acted on what they knew about God's love for them in Jesus. This should not cause us to be fearful for children's prayers for healing – their faith is often stronger than ours anyway!

Other gifts

Let me say again that list of supernatural gifts of the Holy Spirit in 1 Corinthians 12 is not exhaustive. There are other gifts. My detailed explanation of the outworking of the supernatural gifts in children is not intended to imply that any other gifts are inferior in any way. While giving some practical advice on helping children to see the relevance of these particular manifestations of the Holy Spirit, I wish to make the point that their supernatural nature can be a tremendous encouragement to children who are bombarded with ideas that God is merely some kind of 'idea in your head'. Other gifts from the Holy Spirit also need recognising and developing in children, for they are all given '... to prepare God's people for works of service, so that the body of Christ may be built up until we all reach unity in the faith and in the knowledge of the Son of God and become mature, attaining to the whole measure of the fullness of Christ' (Eph. 4:12,13).

10

Growing in faith – the importance of worship

The organist was really enjoying himself – the stops were out and the congregation were singing their hearts out, except, that is, for most of the children. Some were sitting, swinging their legs, looking at some of the hymns in the book – why didn't they sing these ones? It was clear that they weren't sung, because these pages were clean, and obviously had not been turned by human fingers for a long time, if at all. Other children were standing, watching the worship leader, who, although singing the words, obviously had his mind on something else. Still others were just generally looking round, to see who else was there, or at anything else that looked vaguely interesting. Some, however, were singing (including the choristers) and were enjoying it. Others were not sure of the words, but were singing the tune anyway.

A short while later, after some talk, there was 'the children's song'. The organist left his place behind the curtain in the sanctuary and came bustling round to the piano. One of the Sunday School teachers came and stood nearby, with a nylon-strung guitar around her neck. The children perked up at this activity – here at least would be a song they knew. However, their joy soon faded, for the service leader was encouraging everyone to join in the actions – and as the thin sound of the slightly out-of-tune piano and guitar began, even their parents began to wave their arms and move their bodies in a way they never did at any other time! How embarrassing! Still, it was only one song, and now it was time to pray. The children dropped quickly out of sight in the pews. Even the choristers enjoyed this break. They could not be seen by the organist, and sweets were passed round, ready for the sermon. One or two got their comics out, and one even showed off his new computer game, even if the sound meant that it could not actually be played.

Some of the other children in the congregation were not so lucky. The presence of parents or other adults meant that they just had to put up with it. It would not take too long, however, and soon they would be released and allowed to go to their own activities.

The details may vary, but as far as children and worship are concerned, the scenario is very familiar, even if I have taken it to the extreme. Fortunately, I know of many exceptions. Worship does not need to be an endurance test for children.

I have always been an Anglican, and being a chorister from a young age has meant that I have a real love for liturgy and worship. That love and appreciation naturally grew when my faith came alive and worship was transformed from 'something one does well' to an encounter with my Lord and Saviour. The experience of the Holy Spirit added yet another dimension, and having tasted worship that draws the congregation into the felt presence of God, I am not satisfied with anything else! Over the years I have had the opportunity to taste the worship of other denominations, as well as the variety of traditions within the Church of England. I have come to understand that there can never be just one definitive way of worship, and that each church fellowship must work hard to do what it does well, while offering some variety to those within its membership – and those who have yet to join.

In my early years as a Church Army officer, I studied the 'science' of church growth, and I understood that relevant worship is one of the essential ingredients in growing churches. 'People must know that the most high God is also the most nigh God,' wrote Eddie Gibbs reflecting on his observations of growing churches in South America.[1]

This is as true for children as for adults. To love God and worship Him is our prime duty, and we have an obligation to enable this for children.

God wants children to be a part of the worship experience, because they, too, are called to love and worship Him. In Exodus 10:8,9 it is recorded that Moses wanted the children to join the worship in the wilderness. Rightly or wrongly, Pharaoh suspected another motive, but Moses was insistent. In the New Testament, when Jesus entered the temple and upset the tables of the money-changers, and then healed the blind and the lame who came to Him, it was the children who began to shout, 'Hosanna to the Son of David!' Why were the chief priests and teachers of the law so indignant? Was it because of what the children were shouting? Were the children simply copying the praise of the adults who had followed Jesus as He entered Jerusalem on the donkey, or were they inspired by the Holy Spirit to know that Jesus was indeed the promised Messiah, because they could see what He was doing with those Jesus healed? Jesus had already acknowledged that the Father revealed such things to little children – things that seemed hidden from the wise and learned (Matt. 11:25). In the temple Jesus' response was to remind these critical religious superiors of what the Psalmist had written (Ps. 8:2; Matt. 21:16).

In my limited experience, when children see God at work they still get excited and want to give praise to Him! Perhaps the problem is that often they do not see God doing anything. Children have not learnt the social graces, and they don't pretend God is there when they feel He isn't! That is not to say they are always right, of course. We may be aware of the more undramatic work of God, but we must be aware of making excuses for the things we are not seeing but rather hope we do.

Definitions

Again, we must define our terms. In current parlance, it is customary in evangelical/charismatic churches to use the word 'worship' as a synonym for 'singing'. 'Let's have some worship' actually means 'Let's sing'. Sadly, there are many who actually do believe that worship is singing, and consequently the services lack some of the richness and variety that other traditions enjoy.

'Religion that God our Father accepts as pure and faultless is this: to look after orphans and widows in their distress, and to keep oneself from being polluted by the world' (Jas. 1:27). Some commentators point out that the Greek word for 'religion' in this verse may also be translated as 'worship'. True worship is a lifestyle: a lifestyle of service to God. It is no accident that the church meets for a worship *service*, for we meet to serve our God. Meeting with Him and giving Him praise and honour is the prime object, yet, for many Christians, worship is simply the prelude to what we will receive, be it some good teaching, or the spiritual nurture of our souls through the sacrament of Holy Communion. Thus many worship for what they can get out of it, rather than what they can give to it.

This seems to be a far cry from St Paul's idea of worship: 'When you come together, everyone has a hymn, or a word of instruction, a revelation, a tongue or an interpretation. All of these must be done for the strengthening of the church' (1 Cor. 14:26).

Thus every element of a service must be included in worship – even the notices! For those who feel I jest about that, I hasten to affirm that the church notices should be just as much part of our worship as anything else. How can this be? Bishop Colin Buchanan has said: 'Worship is relating to God in the company of others, and relating to others in the presence of God.' This has helped me to understand the relationship between myself and others in worship, and to understand that my interaction with them is an important ingredient of what we give to God. Thus if notices are a necessary part of the meeting together of the family of God, then they need to be carefully prepared to encourage and advise each other – 'relating to others in the presence of God'.

Another helpful understanding can be gained from remembering the words of Jesus: 'God is Spirit, and His worshippers must worship in spirit and in truth' (John 4:24).

Real worship is spiritual and true. It is spiritual because:

- it relates to and involves the human spirit – the heart and will (Rom. 12:1). True worship may move my emotions and my intellect, but it must also challenge my will.
- it relates to and involves the Holy Spirit. He must be involved, and therefore worship may be supernatural and heighten my sense of the numinous – the awesome presence of Almighty God.

Worship is true because:

- it relates to the truth about God. We worship not because we feel like it, but because of who He is. He has revealed Himself through the Bible and in creation itself. He is not dependent on our concept of Him.
- it relates to the truth about ourselves. There is no falsehood when we are in the presence of God. As Anglicans pray at

the beginning of the Holy Communion service, 'Almighty God to whom all hearts are open, and from whom no secrets are hidden . . .' We must be honest with God and with ourselves in worship. We may fool each other, and even fool ourselves, but we cannot fool God – He knows our innermost thoughts and feelings, and whether we 'honour God with our lips, when our hearts are far from Him' (see Matt. 15:8).

Such experience of worship often takes time and needs adequate preparation. Again, this is as true for children as for adults. This phrase keeps occurring because whilst many adults may fully accept these principles, few have thought of applying them to children in the Church. But let us now move to some of the practicalities.

Making the most of Sundays

Whatever the practice of our church, we must make the most of it.

'. . . Children ought to learn about Christ in the context of the Christian community at worship.'[2] This is the conclusion of the working party concerned for the vast majority of children in England who have little or no meaningful contact with the Church. However, this is more easily said than done in many cases. There has been more anguish over children and adults together in worship than over many other issues in the Church. Over and over again I encounter deep dissatisfaction in adults in particular. That is not to say that children do not also feel dissatisfied, it is just that, as is so often the case, their opinion is not really sought or considered.

The main problem seems to be that in many cases what happens is either a children's service with adults present, or an adult service with children present. In any case, what is 'served' is not a good example of the best that happens when children worship or when adults worship. Another significant factor is that some of the children present are not there out of choice, but rather because they have to be there. (The same may be true of a few adults, of course!) Such children then demand a high 'entertainment' factor to keep them amused, otherwise they make their parents regret forcing them to come!

This may be seen in the case of some very young children. A small child soon learns that if they make a big enough noise, pressure will be put upon Mum or Dad to *do* something. Often the child will be taken out to a room where there are toys to play with, a much better place than that boring room where there is nothing to do except stand up, sit down and be quiet! And if Mum or Dad wants to leave and go back in, all the child has to do is yell again! If the church has an organised crèche, this is not so bad, and Mum and Dad can worship with a clear conscience, but the child learns little about worship.

Incidentally, some have suggested that the way to handle the crying child syndrome is to take the child out of the service to quieten down, but then to go back in. The reasoning goes that the child soon learns that nothing is gained by making such a noise. The parents should, however, develop other strategies for enabling the child to stay in the service, bearing in mind the particular needs of that age group.

Without a doubt, there are problems with all-age worship, but I believe that in general they are solvable. One of the first issues to be decided is the purpose of such worship. Some churches have come to the conclusion that Sunday worship is a celebration time in the context of the whole church family together. Teaching is not a major function of that time together, although the biblical content of the worship is ensured. For such churches, teaching within age groups is done on other (mid-week) occasions. However, some fellowships feel that their main purpose on Sundays is to provide a complete 'diet' of worship and, in particular, instruction. This, they believe, cannot be achieved in all-age worship, and so often adults and children only meet together for major festivals. Many other churches work on a compromise, in which children and adults meet in their separate groups, but join for all-age worship for part of the time.

A common practice is to have a monthly family service. During my ministry as a Church Army evangelist I have observed the following responses to such a tradition:

- It does not readily attract people without a family – in other words, the word 'family' is not interpreted as meaning 'all-age'.
- Many children and children's leaders regard it as a 'day off' and rarely come to it.
- Although children are present and often well accommodated, the real goal of the service is to win fringe parents for Christ. In this case, the children are more a means to an end. As Bishop Gavin Reid has commented, such a policy means that many children will have no real chance of their own to meet with God.
- Where such services generally are successful in attracting the target congregation, few of the fringe adults make the jump to the 'normal' church worship. I have, however, seen a significant change in this in churches which are involved in the popular 'Alpha' courses, where the next step is a series of informal meetings around a meal, rather than any kind of commitment to a regular church service.
- Such services generally do not attract new children on their own, except where they are part of an integrated plan of outreach in a local primary school. Children are generally attracted to the regular children's ministry by other children.

- Many adults like the family service because they can understand the sermons. Because of the presence of children, such services involve varied teaching aids – visual and/or dramatic – in order to convey effectively a particular (often simple) biblical truth. But when adults are by themselves, churches resort to the most inefficient teaching method of 'I speak – you listen', with the preacher giving a message far too complex for this medium. Little wonder that interested adults are put off!

These are simply observations and personal comments. I feel that the monthly family service can be (and has often been) effective in some circumstances, though I would always recommend re-naming such a service to avoid the problem of interpretation of that word 'family'.

For the churches that perceive their main problem as being that of adequately teaching such a wide age range, there are the following models: first, all ages stay together, with the children having a talk suitably geared to their age range. Then, whilst the children are invited to complete some kind of worksheet based on the talk, the adults are addressed on the same subject at a more appropriate level.

The second model might be where everyone is together until the adult talk, when the children go out to do a teaching activity appropriate to their age, etc. Time is an important factor in this, especially if the children are to rejoin the adults for the remainder of the service.

A further alternative may be for worship to happen together, but to divide for 'all-age education'. This acknowledges that adults are also at different learning stages in their Christian life, and that they too differ in the ways in which they can best learn and be 'discipled'. In such a scheme adults and children will be involved in different learning activities such as thematic seminars or practical workshops. While some will be geared to specific age groups, some will be for all ages together. In churches with this scheme, in-depth learning is likely to be reserved for mid-week meetings. I believe there is a lot of mileage in this approach, but it is obvious that such a scheme would require flexible premises and sufficient leaders with suitable skills, often not available to the majority of churches.

Harking back to the United Reformed Church's discussion document, *Towards a Charter for Children in the Church*, I would spotlight this challenging proposition:

> As a church community we must learn to do only those things in separate age groups which we cannot in all conscience do together.

The problem is that many congregations do not want to learn – they want an instant answer, hence the number of books and articles on the subject. I am frequently asked if I know of a particular pattern of all-age worship that works. My answer is always to say that there are different models, but there is no universal service that will work for everyone, everywhere. All we can do is to gain clues and ideas. In the end, a congregation has to learn together, and that learning process may take a long time.

Worship is such a sensitive area that many adults feel threatened by the tastes of today's children and young people. Children are welcome as long as they are just like us! However, just as a family may join together in activities because they love each other and are happy to give pleasure to the other members of the family, so it would seem possible for this to happen within the family of the Church. It is not easy to love someone one does not know, and so it seems obvious that we need to help the different age groups to get to know each other. I would advise leaders to develop events and activities outside of worship that enable relationships to develop between those different groups. Those relationships may then be brought into joint worship. When different groups within a congregation know and respect each other, a degree of tolerance may develop to enable genuine all-age worship to grow.

Another (often unspoken) objective of all-age worship may be to hand on the traditions of the denomination to the next generation. This may seem especially important where so many children's groups have few denominational characteristics. They are so broadly (evangelical) Christian that the children often feel unable to relate to the normal worship of the church when the time comes for them to leave and join the adult congregation. In examining issues such as this, some Christians in Australia came to the conclusion that children need to be trained to worship as Anglicans/Methodists/Congregationalists, etc. from an early age. They recommend that all-age worship should simply be the normal worship of the church, with no children's talk or specifically children's music. There is logic behind some of their thinking, and I believe that each denomination has something to offer to the great kaleidoscope that is the Christian Church, and that we should seek to share those gifts with our children. However, I also believe that each denomination must wrestle with the fact that we need to allow the next generation of Christians to bring their insights and cultural contributions to the life of the Church. When it comes to reaching the huge number of unchurched people in our land, we must also acknowledge a potential barrier that is our 'church culture'. As I often point out, where else do people gather to sit on hard benches, where else are there ritual customs of standing and sitting, and where else do certain officials wear unusual clothing? In England, the only comparable place is in court – another ancient institution!

So far I have addressed the worship of children in the context of all-age worship. I would like to move now to looking more specifically at how children worship.

Children in worship

'From the lips of children and infants you have ordained praise, because of your enemies, to silence the foe and the avenger' (Ps. 8:2).

This is the Scripture quoted by Jesus in the temple, when children were shouting His praise, to the indignation of the chief priests and teachers of the law. It is a remarkable verse, for it seems to indicate that children's praise is not only part of God's plan, but even part of spiritual warfare.

'Children have a natural ability to praise and worship, but, as is so often the case, the environment and the influence of adults have encouraged the children to grow up in a way that tends to squeeze this heartfelt expression out of their little lives.'[3]

Even if there is a natural ability, children still need to be taught to worship. Bearing in mind the comments made earlier, we need to teach them what worship is about, and how to enjoy the worship adventure. Too many adults squeeze children into one of two boxes – either that children should be 'just like us', so that proper worship is to worship as adults do, or that children's worship is simply a matter of getting the children to sing a lot of action songs, vaguely connected with the theme of the meeting. Certainly children have a lot of energy, and they are quick to worship with their bodies as well as their mouths (unless they have already learnt, perhaps from inhibited parents, that such behaviour is embarrassing or unseemly). However, children are also capable of intimate worship when suitably motivated, and more suitable songs of adoration are being written for use by children.

Leading children in worship

The first requirement in leading children in worship is that the leader has a right relationship with God. This seems obvious, but I have seen over and over again that the principles that adults apply to adult worship are seldom seen as totally necessary with children! Thus I state the obvious: the worship leader must primarily be a worshipper, in love with Jesus and filled with the Holy Spirit. If he/she is to lead others into the presence of God, then the leader must cultivate that intimacy and constant song of praise in the heart – 'overflowing with thankfulness' as St Paul puts it (Col. 2:7).

If a leader has a right relationship with God, he/she must also have a right attitude to children. The worship leader must like children as well as love them, and must see him/herself as a servant of the children, as well as a leader. Jesus Himself said, 'I am among you as one who serves' (Luke 22:27). He is our model. In a right sense, too, the leader is also a model, and invites the children to imitate him or her; see 1 Corinthians 4:16. We should not fight shy of this role, whilst asking God's help in remaining humble. As one father said to me, 'My children are going to have their heroes anyway, so I would much rather they were Christian ones, rather than the alternatives the world has to offer!' What does the leader model? In this case it is a living relationship with God, and the ability to worship and respond to God.

A worship leader commits quality time to preparation, praying about the theme of the meeting and the needs of the age range. Careful choice of songs is made, bearing in mind the purpose of the songs, whether they are to lead the children into God's presence, if they are to help children to get into a right relationship with God, if they are to reinforce the teaching or to recap on last week's topic, etc. The task may well be to cover all of these aims – an impossible task in the space of three songs! There would normally be a sense of moving into God's presence from objective praise and thanksgiving, preparing to meet with Him in adoration, in confession, in intercession and in simple receiving from our heavenly Father.

As with any journey, the children can only begin where they are. When the leader stands to begin the worship, one of his/her initial tasks is to identify that place and begin the process of enabling the children to meet with God in worship. This generally means starting with bright songs that may have more of a fun element than theological content, moving to songs with more objective truths about God and about children. All of these may have actions, but they are not absolutely necessary all the time. Active participation does enable the non-singers to be involved, and can harness the natural energy and noisiness of the junior-age child. Actions can also enhance the meaning of a children's song, they are not just actions for sake of having actions. Be aware, also, that not all children are the same, and that variety is as helpful to children as it is to adults.

So there should be a sense of movement, moving from songs about God to songs that speak to Him, that express simple response to His love for His children. In some cases, this could be in a block of worship songs, with few, if any, introductions, letting the songs speak for themselves, and allowing the Holy Spirit to move. Children may be encouraged to close their eyes if they know the words, and concentrate on singing to Jesus. In some cases, it may be appropriate to encourage singing with words the Holy Spirit gives. However, we should beware of getting into a routine that has this 'downward curve', as worship leaders often describe it. There should be a freedom to move in and out of joyful praise and quiet worship, while being sensitive to the leading of the Holy Spirit. Remember, though, that familiarity and predictability are helpful to children, because they can relax and stay tuned in more to the Holy Spirit, rather than be anxious about what is going to happen next. Another easy trap into which worship leaders may easily fall is to be so caught up in worship ourselves that we forget the children, and leave them behind!

Familiar prayers and Scripture responses may be part of this worship adventure, leading us into a divine encounter. Children should be encouraged to act out their role in the 'priesthood of all believers' (1 Pet. 2:5,9) in careful intercession. This, like all other things, can be taught and encouraged. Styles and topics should vary, whilst developing effective methods for your particular group of children.

Bible readings may be left until the lesson time, but I would generally encourage a time of quiet, if it is appropriate. Of course, it may also be one of those days when the children don't get very far on the journey. Don't be too discouraged by this unless it happens regularly. In that case, try and talk with the children in small groups to find out why it isn't working for them. It may be you, the worship leader, but it may equally be some other factor you have overlooked.

May I summarise some of my strongest feelings about children and worship:

Needs for children's worship

Children need anointed worship leaders, sensitive to the leading of God the Holy Spirit, sensitive to the children present – and sensitive to the clock! Children need to know that someone is in control, someone who loves them and loves God. This gives a sense of security and freedom to relax. The subject of anointing is an interesting one. What does it mean? My own definition is that God's anointing is visible from the nature and effectiveness of someone's ministry. A natural gift or skill may be anointed, and become a gift of the Holy Spirit in a real sense, when it is done in God's power, at God's inspiration, for God's glory. To lead worship is more than the ability to choose songs and introduce them. It requires a sensitivity to the Holy Spirit, and a boldness to lead others. It is worth noting that such an anointing may be on some youngsters, as well as/rather than adults.

Children need to be led into worship. As we have already discussed, worship is a response to a real experience of God in our lives. When we meet together for worship, children (and adults) need to be motivated to do so. It may take time to get to that stage of worshipping from our hearts and not just from our lips. This may be because of the lack of preparation, mentioned earlier, though it may be because of demonic pressure. Children as much as adults can pick up all sorts of demonic influences, just like picking up a virus! I realise that not everyone will agree with this view of the enemy and all his works, but I have often realised the need to engage in quiet spiritual warfare, in order to free the children to give true worship to God.

Children need excellence in music. Why should the adults have the best musicians? In the majority of churches there is an assumption that the best musicians should be involved in adult worship. In one church I know there are two adult worship teams, yet only one or two others who will commit themselves to helping the children to worship. Those in the adult worship bands are reluctant to get involved with the children, and there has been little encouragement from the church leadership to do so. In the past we have had an excellent record in teaching musical skills in our schools – a situation already changing, as music teachers are victims of educational cost-cutting. However, for now, there are often talented child musicians in our churches. The main problem is how to use the inevitable variety of instruments to form a worship band and lead the children in quality worship.

Another observation I have made is that children's musicians do not generally spend as much time in rehearsal as does the adult worship group. Why is this? Is it the fact that 'they are only children'?

If there is a problem with getting capable musicians for the children's work, I would always suggest the use of recorded music. Many songs are now available as 'backing tracks', but it is easy enough to produce one's own, by getting friendly musicians to record them! If these are copied on to short, five-minute cassettes (the type which used to be sold as computer tapes), one song to a cassette, duplicated on each side, they become a very usable resource. The usual copyright conditions will apply, of course.[4]

Children need to be able to worship in a way that is relevant to them. There is an increasing repertoire of good children's music, but the problem is locating it. A visit to the local Christian bookshop should help, and Christian magazines often have reviews of the latest productions. A good children's work leader will also keep an eye (ear?) on what is being sung at the local schools, and indeed, may be appreciated if he/she has some suggestions for the school.

Worship is not just singing, as I have said earlier. There is a lot of scope in developing the spoken word in relevant worship for children. I will deal with this in more detail in the next chapter.

Children need to be reminded of their Christian heritage in the hymns we love and cherish – but we need to remember they reflect a culture that is often quite different or alien to today's child.

The rapid expansion of the modern worship song has, in some cases, led to the demise of the traditional hymn. There are many children who know no hymns, for they are often not even sung in schools. I believe this to be a case of 'throwing the baby out with the bath-water', and we are in danger of losing some of our Christian heritage. Many of our best-loved hymns represent a culture that is foreign to many children, because of the rhythm, the metre and, often, the way they are played. Some churches emphasise the difference by consistently letting the organ play the hymns and the music group the songs. Surely it is possible to blur the distinctions? I also realise that the guitar is not the best instrument for playing many hymns, and this immediately limits the scope of worship in some children's groups, where there are no other more suitable instruments. The home-grown 'backing tracks' mentioned earlier may be appropriate here.

I am also aware of the place of 'home-grown' music, and would encourage more people to consider writing new songs. They may not be included in the next edition of your favourite hymn-book, but may be 'songs for a season' – similar to contemporary prophecy. By this I mean that they represent what God is saying now into your church's situation, a situation that may only be temporary. I have written several songs that fit into that category – effective sung once, then no longer relevant.

Children's worship is generally honest, and much more fun. It may take more work to complete the worship journey, as children are not pretenders, but it is well worth the effort. The times of quiet intimacy may be shorter, but they are no less meaningful. We are training children in patterns of worship that will last them a lifetime, but we must always be encouraging them to grow in worship, leading them on to the next stage. The late Revd David Watson wrote, 'If we neglect our foremost calling [i.e. worship], we become spiritually arid in ourselves, we have nothing of lasting value to offer the world, and we dishonour God.'[5] True worship is an essential resource for the growth – and ministry – of a Christian disciple of any age.

11

Growing in faith – good worship for all ages

How can churches move ahead in all-age worship? What contribution can be made to such worship by those who have an experience of the power and ministry of, and in, the Holy Spirit? These are the issues I would now like to explore.

Preparation

When my wife and I were invited (as Church Army officers) to one of the Queen's garden parties at Buckingham Palace, we spent a lot of time and care in getting ourselves ready. The fact that we would be among at least a thousand others and unlikely actually to meet Her Majesty was irrelevant. The occasion demanded that we look our very best.

If meeting with our Queen required such preparation, how much more should our meeting with the King of kings? Local tradition may dictate on such things as clothing, but with children as with adults, I need to give attention to preparing them to meet with God. As a young Christian, I was taught to prepare myself before leaving home (even if I seldom did it), and in church and Sunday School there was a reverent quietness before worship commenced. All this enhanced a feeling that this was a special time, a different time. Even for many adults now, however, that time before the beginning of a service consists of loud conversation in competition with the organist or music group.

If, because of busy lifestyles, people generally do not prepare themselves to worship, then I suggest we must make time for such preparation when the service has technically begun. Sometimes the opening music can achieve this, especially if there can be a number of items that the Holy Spirit can use to enable the congregation to worship 'in Spirit and in Truth'. Alternatively, it may simply be a case of addressing the children in such words as, 'Now before we begin to worship God through our singing, let us be quiet for just a moment. Picture yourself in the garden of a house. Inside, Jesus is there and you want to go in to meet Him. Ask the Holy Spirit to help you get ready, so that Jesus will like you being there, and that you will know what to say to Him and His friends.'

This may not seem such a revolutionary step forward in all-age worship, but as a worship leader I recommend you give the subject serious consideration.

What other ways can you think of to prepare children for worship?

What are the hurdles that prevent such a reverent preparation?

Is the natural noisiness and energy of children such a hurdle?

Planning

'Renewed worship also embraces both planning and spontaneity . . . However, worship should not be so pre-planned as to allow no room for the *living* God to speak to us in an unexpected way.'[1]

When planning all-age worship, the language ability of the congregation needs to be taken into account. When small children are present, it is important they understand some of the basic ingredients. It is not necessary to bring every-thing down to a low common denominator – the spoken word, like the sung word, can be more relevant to different groups within the congregation at different times. Different groups can be 'stretched' by being invited to 'listen in' on a topic that is more pertinent to another group within the church. We should not be afraid of what might be termed 'Christian jargon', but we must ensure the congregation understands what we are talking about! Another simple word of practical advice is about including children in what is being said. In this country, I believe that in a mixed (all-age) group, when an adult speaks, children automatically assume it is the adults who are being addressed. I think this is because children are generally ignored when adults get together at home or wherever, and so they bring the same expectations into church. The worship leader needs to men-tion the children particularly, if they are included in the comments or instructions. Similarly, at points of the service which are more relevant to adults – a rather lengthy Bible reading that is not a story, for instance – one can say something like, 'Children, this Bible reading may not be easy for you to follow, and the adults will get more out of it. However, look out for this particular word, and see how many times it is mentioned.'

Adults and children alike enjoy familiar patterns in wor-ship, but variety within the familiar pattern is essential to stimulate fresh interest. Liturgy is a skeleton rather than a straitjacket. We should feel free to experiment within limits, building on what works without overkilling that particular element. For this reason, it is helpful for someone to have oversight of such worship to ensure this variety, while not losing sight of the effective elements, so that lessons are not forgotten.

If familiar patterns are helpful, good, anointed leadership is essential. The ability to communicate to all ages is not easy. It can be learned, but as with other aspects of ministry, it is best to seek those who have a clear spiritual anointing in this area. It may be necessary to share leadership of all-age worship between those able to communicate with children and those whose gifting is with adults. Where a service may be largely unstructured it is especially important to have leadership that is recognised and trusted, otherwise a congregation may feel rather insecure.

Time constraints are also important. Children generally have much shorter spans of concentration than adults. While there are anointed preachers who can hold even children for thirty to forty minutes, most of us do not have such an anointing and may struggle to hold even adults for that length of time. In addition, other physical conditions make a congregation aware of time – hard seats, cold (or hot) temperature, imminent meal times. To have a time limit does not necessarily mean 'quenching the Spirit'. It is nearly always possible to have a formal ending to the service, but to allow further time for those who need more time for receiving from, or responding to, God. There is always another week, as well!

Ingredients of worship

Good worship (all-age or otherwise) must have a balance of music, the spoken word (both of which will involve Scripture), silence, fellowship and receiving (often called 'ministry').

Music. I am convinced about the extreme importance of music in worship, while never claiming that it is essential. Music communicates to the soul – we feel it much more than mere words. It is also a kind of universal language. Another fact is that church members (children included) learn most of their theology from what they sing. This is simply because of repetition. As a child I learnt my 'times tables' by repeating them, parrot fashion, along with all the others in my class. I have never forgotten them.

Whereas relatively few church members are able to recite any verses of Scripture from memory, most are able to sing several verses of a number of hymns with ease. The modern worship song (often erroneously called a 'chorus') is usually simple, easy to understand and easy to sing, and therefore suitable for all age groups. However, some worship songs have imagery that is not very relevant to children. There is also the problem that the great majority of modern worship songs are very subjective, and are more concerned with our response to God than the objective truths about Him. In this area, I am pleased that many of the children's songs still contain much of this objective content, while more are being written to enable children to respond to what God is revealing about Himself, in ways that are appropriate to children, not adults.

We should not be afraid of introducing new songs (or old songs to different groups within the church), but we should be careful about how often we exercise the congregation in this way. I often saw the reality of this when I was a regular worship leader. We sought to keep abreast of the main developments in modern worship songs, and kept an eye on how many we were introducing each month. However, when a 'golden oldie' was sung the volume and intensity often increased, because people could relax in what they were singing, without having to work at it. I have also seen this to be true with children. We have a lot of excellent modern Christian music being written and recorded in this country (for children as well as adults), and more people could be encouraged to buy a Christian album of some kind once or twice a year. In this way also the repertoire could be encouraged to grow.

One of the recent developments in charismatic worship is the pattern of having a block of worship songs without any break, allowing the songs to speak for themselves, rather than having an announcement or introduction from the worship leader. Many of us find this helpful in worship, but such blocks can be very long for children. A sensitive worship leader will be as much aware of the children as the adults in this.

In the previous chapter I remarked on the demise of the traditional hymn. I am concerned that we keep a broad diet, of styles as well as length and subject, of the hymns and songs we sing. This demands a lot of a worship leader, and those with such a breadth of awareness and knowledge are rare. This is another case for shared responsibility in seeking a healthy diet of sung worship, by gathering together, at regular intervals, a group of worship 'advisors' who can pool their knowledge of suitable music.

The Holy Spirit is the agent of creation and creativity, but He seems to be quenched in our dependence on musical instruments. In one church, when there was a power failure, it was suggested that we should abandon the hymns, as the piano was out of tune! I would encourage churches to experiment more with songs without the organ or band, encouraging spontaneous harmony. This requires courageous leadership, but is often very rewarding. Similarly we should not be afraid of using instrumental music. Our services are often so busy that an organ voluntary or guitar and flute duet can provide wonderful space for thought and prayer – or a cause for praise. Instrumental music can be very powerful when used as a background to prayers or readings from Scripture. This does not necessarily demand live music, and good quality reproduction can make the use of recorded music very easy and acceptable. I might also add here that some Christians feel that Christian music is the only appropriate music in worship. By this, they often mean it has a Christian title, or is an instrumental version of a Christian hymn or song. I differ on this interpretation, for I believe music is a neutral medium, which can be used for good or evil. I suspect that some Christians are afraid of their emotional response to some rhythms and tunes, just as some are equally uncomfortable with some aspects of dance in worship. Like most things of this nature, such creativity requires careful preparation, and it would be most helpful if the responsibility could be shared amongst the leadership.

Finally, I would like to recommend the regular use of singing in, or with, the Holy Spirit. St Paul said, 'I will sing with my spirit, but I will also sing with my mind' (1 Cor. 14:15). This includes what is called prophetic worship as well as singing in tongues. There is great power in singing in tongues, and I know of one church that allows for this at a particular moment in the weekly Sunday morning liturgy. I have come to understand that just as I need no ecstatic moment to speak in tongues, there is equally no need for such a moment in order to sing in tongues. This does not deny those particular times when the Holy Spirit comes especially close and a whole congregation is caught up in supernatural worship of a special kind.

I also believe that such an activity can be introduced without making anyone feel left out, especially those who are not able, for any reason, to speak in tongues. One can sing spontaneously in English as much as in tongues, and this may still be singing in the Spirit. Any who might still feel excluded can be invited simply to listen and to pray, to see if the Holy Spirit might manifest His presence in some other way. I have often introduced this practice by calling it spontaneous singing, rather than singing in the Spirit. This may overcome a natural fear that some people have, and enable them to have an experience of the Holy Spirit otherwise denied them.

Consider the music at your church. Who is responsible for choosing it? Consider an all-age musical survey which will enable you to discover what people like to sing and why.

What hymns are known and sung by the children in your church? Are there others that you feel should be in their repertoire? How can they be introduced and 'sold' to the children?

What use is made of instrumental music, if any? What initial steps can you take to be creative in this way?

Spoken word. Just as singers can become dependent on instruments, worshippers can become dependent on music. Whilst I fully acknowledge the value of music in worship, I am also keen on the use of the spoken word. Here again the Holy Spirit can inspire great creativity. The Church of England has seen rapid developments in prayer-book revision over recent years – not without controversy. Official and unofficial publications have given inspiration for fresh liturgy. Many Christians are unhappy with the repetitive nature of liturgical responses, feeling that such repetition causes a loss of real meaning. I believe this underestimates the activity of the Holy Spirit. Liturgy is simply recited Scripture, and surely the rehearsal of Scripture is no bad thing!

When Terry Waite was in captivity, the fact that he was able to recite the daily office and verses of Scripture was, he claims, one of the things that enabled him to survive his long period of confinement.

For those churches whose worship would not be regarded as 'liturgical', I believe creative use of the spoken word could enhance their worship. I suggest that churches develop several alternatives, while not having too many. Thus they may be learnt by heart, just like a song. Experiment with rhythm to accompany responsive Scripture (called versicles and responses in the Church of England). The rhythm can be by hand clapping or on drums (though I have used the drum section of an electronic keyboard as an alternative!). Treat such a thing as one would a song. Repeat it once or twice, but not to the point of boredom.

Yet another use of the spoken word is through choral reading. This is another way of using the Bible in worship. It may be described as a song without a tune. Again, it takes time to prepare, but the result can be very effective. Just as a dramatic reading would take a Bible story and assign various voices to the different characters, the narrator, etc., so a choral reading is a way of giving voices to different parts of a prose passage, such as a Psalm or a section of one of the New Testament letters. The use of an overhead projector can enable the whole congregation to take part; otherwise it may be spoken by a group of readers. For instance, let us take a passage from St Paul's letter to the Colossians, chapter 1:

v.10: . . . we pray . . . in order that you may live a life worthy of the Lord and may please him in every way: *bearing fruit in every good work*, growing in the knowledge of God, v.11: being strengthened with all **power** according to his glorious might so that you may have great endurance *and patience*, and joyfully

v.12: giving thanks to the Father, who has qualified you to share in the inheritance of the saints in the kingdom of light.

v.13: *For he has rescued us from the dominion of darkness* and brought us into the kingdom of the Son he loves,

v.14: *in whom we have redemption*, **the forgiveness of sins**.

v.15: He is the image of the invisible God, the firstborn over all creation.

v.16: *For by him all things were created*: things in heaven and on earth, *visible and invisible*, whether thrones or powers or rulers or authorities; **all things were created by him and for him**.

v. 17: *He is before all things, and in him all things hold together.*

v.18: And he is the head of the body, the church; *he is the beginning and the firstborn from among the dead*, **so that in everything he might have the supremacy**.

v.19: For God was pleased to have all his fullness dwell in him,

v.20: *and through him to reconcile to himself all things*, whether things on earth *or things in heaven*, by making peace **through his blood**, shed on the cross.

I have sought to interpret the passage for two groups of voices. The idea is that one group says the words in italic, the other the words in normal type, and both groups say the words printed in bold. There can be solo voices, paying attention to whether they are deep or high pitched, etc. Such a passage may have instrumental music in the background, to add impact.

The spoken word also includes prayer, though prayer can also be musical. Just as song-writers have worked hard to craft some of the beautiful worship songs and hymns we love, we should not neglect the prayers written with similar time and effort. There is a place for the written prayer and the extempore prayer. Prayers learnt as a child can be a source of strength and inspiration for a lifetime.

We should be especially careful to be imaginative and creative with intercessions where children are present. It is often possible to have visual aids for intercessions – not an impossible task for these days of 'desk top publishing' on home computers. Unless they are able to follow the prayer in some way, prayers should be relatively short. I also tell the children the subject of my prayers to gain their attention and interest. It is important to record answers to prayer, so that children come to understand this is not some kind of meaningless exercise. Prayer in groups can be good, refreshing and helpful, but children generally need to have some practice at this in the children's groups or at home, before being expected to launch forth with a group of relative strangers!

One final comment: there is a great difference between reading out a prayer and praying a prayer! I have often seen children, sometimes with little warning, given written prayers to read out at the time for intercessions in a service. A good reader may seem to do a good job, but I believe those who lead intercessions in any way must *own* their prayers and believe in what they are praying, otherwise it may simply become a literary exercise.

Preaching, teaching and instruction would also be covered by the spoken word in worship. I have already mentioned some aspects of this in the previous chapter, and feel it is inappropriate to say more. Whole books are devoted to the subject; investigate your local Christian bookshop.

How is the spoken word used in your church? How do children respond to liturgy?

How can adults help liturgy to be helpful to children?

Organise an evening workshop to find suitable passages of Scripture for use as opening responsive liturgy, or to find and 'orchestrate' a passage of Scripture for choral reading.

Silence. We live in a noisy world. Many people (including children) have no real experience of silence, and some are uncomfortable or even afraid of it! We generally need to learn to be silent. The art of meditation seems to be the province of a special few. I understand that some work has been done by Roman Catholic sisters in teaching Christian meditation, and this seems to me a much better alternative to the transcendental meditation that is being encouraged by well-meaning, but sadly mistaken adults in the teaching world.

Many adults will be surprised to learn that children can enjoy silence in worship, for it seems to be contrary to their nature. However, in my experience, when there is a purpose behind it, even children can look forward to silence. The problem is that children are most often required to be silent for the sake of the adults, or as some kind of punishment. When taught about the ministry of the Holy Spirit, children, too, can receive spiritual gifts of prophecy and pictures, etc. 'for the common good' (1 Cor. 12:7). We must also be aware of the shorter concentration spans of children, however, and not put our usual adult expectations on them. Their silence may be shorter, but it is no less profound. After such a time, there should be an opportunity for children (and adults) to share anything that God has shown them in that silence, whether it is to be shared with the whole church, or a leader, or within a family group, for instance.

What prevents effective silence being experienced in your church?

What steps can be taken to teach children to expect to hear God or receive from Him when we give Him space?

Fellowship. '. . . relating to others in the presence of God'. I have already mentioned that the notices need not be a bore, and that they can be part of enjoying each other's company. Scripture tells us to sing to each other, pray for each other, build each other up, etc. I am convinced that it is perfectly acceptable to God to have fun together during worship, whilst not allowing it to dominate and divert attention from Him. Fun is not the same as irreverence, but it can easily become so when allowed to run out of control. Our responsibility to each other also means that we must be aware of those who find fun and laughter inappropriate in church.

Fellowship in all-age worship is not just about fun, but it is about relationships. Children are fortunate in having a good number of fun songs, and also songs in which to do simple dances. There are other all-age activities which can occur during worship, and many books have been written on the subject. I would mention two simple ideas: first the old-fashioned testimony, and second refreshments. It is so encouraging to hear other people's faith stories. These need not be about 'when I became a Christian . . .' Most of us need to be encouraged that the little things in our lives are also part of the building blocks used by the Holy Spirit to form us and mould us in Christ's likeness. Thus the testimonies (or stories) of the little things we have discovered and how they have affected us are as important as the dramatic conversion accounts. Children as well as adults can be encouraged to say what God is doing in their lives. Not everyone can stand up and just talk (though it can be encouraged), and so an interview technique can be used. It is a good idea to practise such story-times. This does not remove any spontaneity, it simply honours the congregation in that this, too, needs to be done with skill and excellence to enable the best in worship.

One of the interesting things to happen in the Church of England with the introduction of the Alternative Service Book was the re-introduction of the 'passing of the peace', an ancient custom during the service of Holy Communion. This was not without controversy; as one traditional church-goer was heard to comment, 'I don't come to church to be friendly with folks!' However, this point in the service can have beneficial effects, for it acts as a kind of 'commercial break' to a generation of people who have become used to such interruptions to their television viewing. It allows people to make peace with each other (if they are brave enough to do it during a service), it allows new people to shake hands with others in the church, perhaps even exchanging names. Although some see it as intrusive in worship, I believe it can be a powerful act of fellowship. If your church does not have such a practice, why not simply have a short break, a rest on the worship journey, to relax, to chat, to visit the toilet – even to have some refreshments? This can be valuable in a lengthy service, or even in a normal one where children are present.

> What opportunities for fellowship exist during the worship at your church? What about during all-age worship? Is a break a good idea or a disaster? What about children who would hope it was the end, rather than an intermission?
>
> If a break of some kind is not appropriate, what other things can happen to develop relationships between those in the service?

Receiving and responding.   Worship can be likened to a journey, the destination of which is to restore and refresh our relationship with God, to renew our commitment and to equip us for the work that lies ahead. The encounter with God can be experienced in many different ways, and different parts of the worship can speak and provoke response. There is often an assumption that people will be able to make their own response, but in my experience people need help to take the necessary steps. God speaks to children, too, and so it would seem appropriate to provide opportunities for children as well as adults to respond to what God is saying, in a way that is relevant to their age. It may simply be a time of quiet, when the worship leader asks simple questions: 'What is God saying? What does He want you to do?' We need to give God space to work, to speak, to manifest His presence. However, the worship leaders should bear in mind the fact that children are easily manipulated, and that in the effort to please those they love they will often respond to an invitation to do something.

The response may be combined with an opportunity to receive from God. This is one of the features of recent charismatic worship, when the congregation is invited simply to stand (or sit) and wait on God, ready to receive the good gifts that our heavenly Father longs to give to His children (Matt. 7:11). This is a step of faith that takes God at His word, that knows that God will give to us not because we deserve anything, but because He loves all His children. It has been my pleasure to see children increasingly receive deep things in such times, with some falling to the floor under the power of the Holy Spirit.

I am also of the school of thought that teaches that sometimes 'it is in giving that we receive'. Practically, this means that if after a while I perceive in my spirit that nothing is happening within me, then I look round to see where God is working and join in! In the words often used in such circles, 'we bless what God is doing'. We do not try to make God work where He isn't, but rather follow His lead. This is an ideal opportunity to disciple children, inviting any who feel that God has nothing special for them at this time to join with those who are praying. Ministry team members can quietly point out some of the signs of the Holy Spirit's activity, and encourage the children to join in silent prayer – or even vocal prayer, if they feel they would like to do so. This is an opportunity for hands-on praying described in an earlier chapter.

'Even when worship is a natural overflow of our love for God, it will, and should, cost us something. David once said, "I will not offer to the Lord that which costs me nothing" (see 2 Sam. 24:24). Worship that costs us nothing is worth precisely what it costs!'[2]

Good worship takes a lot of effort. It may take time to

develop, but it is so worth while. It is also true to note that as the church family grows and changes, so will the worship. It will never be a static thing. In worship, too, we are, as someone has said, 'a pilgrim people' – always on the move.

12

Growing in faith – children and groups

Grow in the grace and knowledge of our Lord and Saviour Jesus Christ. To Him be glory both now and for ever! Amen (2 Pet. 3:18).

Growth in understanding is part of the natural maturing of children, and books that deal specifically with teaching children give clear guidance about the different ways in which children learn at each stage. The charts in the appendix were drawn up by Church Army officers, to help children's workers understand the basic characteristics of each age group and how those characteristics may affect our teaching methods. As has been said in an earlier chapter, growth in faith is more than the mental accumulation of Bible facts, and it is this wider dimension of growth that is the focus of this chapter – discipleship for children.

We, as adults, need and enjoy a variety of experiences in learning, ministry and fellowship. Celebrations, small groups, conferences, retreats, seminars, workshops and ministry groups are just some of those experiences. I would suggest that our younger brothers and sisters in Christ may also benefit from such a variety, while remembering that they are not independent, they have no money of their own, they rely on their parents to transport them, etc. We should therefore be realistic in our aims. What kind of groups are achievable in your church? I suggest that most churches will be able to establish some kind of children's housegroups.

Children's housegroups

The adults in our churches are encouraged to attend house-groups, i.e. to belong to a small group where they can safely explore and experience the things of God. Why can't our children do exactly the same? The vision is to see Christian children taking a full part in the life of the Church:

- praying together
- sharing needs with each other
- studying the Bible
- ministering to one another using gifts of the Spirit
- growing in their faith in Jesus

The housegroup setting encourages children in all these things, giving them assurance and confidence in their faith. The small-group setting gives time and individual encourage-ment to explore and experience the things of God. Children aged seven and upwards benefit from housegroups, but the age range in any one group must be within the ability of the leaders. The principles are the same as in adult housegroups, with the practicalities at a child's level. Some churches have replaced their traditional Sunday School by setting up home-groups. As a result, one church reported 100 per cent growth within three months!

What of the practicalities? The following ideas are based on the experience of a large Anglican church in England. They are suggestions only and need to be adapted to each church setting.

How do you set up a housegroup?   The pastor or minister must be fully behind the principles and your aims. Find your leaders. They need to understand the vision, and have had some experience of working with children. Two adults per group of twelve to fifteen children should be adequate.

Where should such a group be held?   Find a suitable home – preferably near the church. This is important if the groups are to coincide with worship in church, but also to establish a firm link with the church. We are not suggesting some kind of rival house church! What makes a home suitable? This will depend on the numbers expected, the kind of behaviour expected by the children (some children may not treat your furniture as well as you usually do!) and the kind of activities you expect to do.

When should the group meetings take place, and how often?   Early evening seems to work best, and about one hour seems long enough. It has been suggested that it is best to give the children an hour after school to let off steam, and to grab some refreshments at home before coming out again to a housegroup. Others, however, have found that it is very practical for children to come straight from school – especially if the venue is near the school. This makes it convenient for transporting children home after the meeting, and may meet with more parental co-operation. Having weekly meetings, during school terms, rather than fortnightly ones helps with continuity. In order to assist the parents, copy a few cards giving the dates of the meetings. A card is better than a paper handout, for it can stand up better, and is not so likely to get mislaid or thrown away. This can be attractively produced by someone with a computer – much better than being written by hand. If the group is an alternative to Sunday groups, then the card can also contain any set themes of the meetings, though it might be more flexible to have a broad theme for the term. You can then take this at the pace set by the children, rather than the material!

Which children should be invited to such a group, and how should they be invited? This depends a lot on the church setting, but ideally it should be Christian children from church families. This helps with fellowship at home and liaison with parents, if needed. However, many non-church children are attracted to such a setting. Perhaps 'evangelistic homegroups' may be organised periodically, with the children doing the inviting and the leading of the group?

Publicise the opportunity in the church and children's group. Explain clearly to the eligible children that it is for those who want to learn more about Jesus. Explain that it will include Bible study, praying, sharing and worship. It is not another 'club' and it is not a games evening, but it is exciting and enjoyable learning together.

If children are interested then talk to the parents. Let the response come from the children, not from the parents thinking their child ought to go to a housegroup. If that is the case the child will probably not stay, or will resent having to come to something they did not choose. It is not an élitist, super-spiritual group. Taking a clue from the Scout and Guide organisations, it may be useful to have some kind of junior leaders, appointed for a term at a time. These will be the equivalent of the church wardens, in a way, and can be given responsibility for practical things such as opening the door as children arrive, making refreshments, etc. As things develop, their responsibility may be stretched to cover other parts of the programme.

What kind of programme should such a housegroup have? There should be some kind of sung and spoken *worship*. It helps to have a keyboard or guitar to encourage the children to worship God together. Some thought will also be needed about words – will the songs be in books, on duplicated sheets, or will you use an overhead projector? There are advantages and disadvantages in each method. Be aware that a small group may make the children rather self-conscious at first. They can hear the sound of their own voice. It may be helpful to have the group 'make a contract' at the beginning about what will be expected of them (including worship), and what they can expect. The children can discuss this, and come to an agreement together. This in itself may be unexpected, as children are so used to having adults make choices for them.

Prayer and *thanksgiving* should be part of the programme. This is an excellent opportunity to train children in open prayer and sharing needs. If your church has a tradition of using prayers from a book, this may be rather difficult, but it is not impossible to develop a blend of written prayers and praying aloud from the heart.

The goal of having everyone praying out of their hearts is one that can be written into the group 'contract'. I suggest you may adopt an apprenticeship model which has been variously used by many others. The training may stretch over several weeks. In reality this means:

1. The leaders pray, acting as good models. Simple, short, honest prayers, with no religious language.
2. The leaders pray, with the children copying, or the leaders suggest the topics and the children pray the prayers which they have written down.
3. The children suggest the topics, and the leaders suggest ways of praying for them. Help the children to understand that a single topic may be prayed about by several people. Encourage them not necessarily to repeat what has been

prayed already, but think of another aspect of the subject. The children then pray, following the suggestions.

4. The children do the praying.

There are the usual teaching points to cover. For instance, that there is no need for special language, though sometimes the beauty of a written prayer may convey a heartfelt cry so well. It doesn't matter if two children speak out at once. It may be embarrassing, but God doesn't mind.

Some suggest that we enable children to opt out of praying aloud by passing an object around. The children can pray if they have the object (a Bible, or whatever) or they can pass it on if they do not wish to pray aloud. I tend to agree that a housegroup is an important training ground, and that there should be an expectation to have everyone pray aloud. I also feel that the housegroup is an excellent opportunity to experiment with different ways of prayer.

Finally, do make a note about prayer requests, and be sure to remind the group of answers to prayer.

Bible teaching should also have some part of the meeting. If this is extra to the normal children's teaching, decide what connection there should be with themes. It may be different, or it may be supplemental, building on what has preceded the housegroup meeting. It should have a practical application relevant to the lives of the children. Encourage all children to bring a Bible, preferably the same version. Perhaps your church has an award scheme that presents each child with a Bible at some stage, when they are moving from one particular group to another? I have always recommended all new Christians to use their own Bible regularly, rather than a church edition. In this way we get to know the relative positions of verses and passages in our particular Bible, even if we forget the actual reference. Children may be encouraged to mark helpful passages or words with a pencil.

Every meeting needs a time for *waiting on God*. Use the groups to enable the children to experience times of quiet, encouraging them to ask God for a picture, or word or Bible verse. The size of the group will affect the manner in which the children can share the things they feel God has given them. If each child in a group of twelve shares for one minute, that may already take up a large proportion of the time available for the group. However, handled sensitively, the group setting gives the children a safe environment to experience and use gifts of the Spirit.

Feedback to parents can often be helpful, e.g. if a particular problem has been shared or a child has spoken out with a Bible verse or picture (it can be a great encouragement to an amazed parent). It is important to get the child's permission to mention it, however.

There should be scope for *ministry*. The housegroup is an excellent opportunity for children to learn to minister to each other, perhaps using the hands-on praying approach. The leader(s) should not be afraid of receiving ministry from children. Be careful not to make it a game, or to patronise children or to use them to meet your needs. Do not expect any kind of instant maturity, and do not forget they are children. The small pastoral group is the usual place to identify giftings, though occasionally, as with Timothy, it comes through prophecy (1 Tim. 1:18) and laying on of hands (2 Tim. 1:6), as mentioned earlier. The practice and development of giftings can also take place within the group. It is best for children to learn to minister to other children before ministering to adults, and so the wider children's group is the next place for ministry to develop outside the small group. As children begin to minister regularly, they need to understand continually the link between the power of the Spirit and the ministry we exercise, seeing the need to 'be filled with the Spirit' every day, and seeking God's special anointing for particular tasks or occasions.

Another training objective of the children's homegroup may be to engage in some kind of *service*. Perhaps there are practical things that the group can do around the church, or in the community. These may be long-term projects, but I suggest initially that they are ones that can be done in a single evening or Saturday morning, etc.

Workshops and ministry groups

It may be that I have not been in the right places, but I am aware of children doing workshops only at large camps or conferences. There is no need for such activities to be restricted to this kind of event. They only require a place to meet and someone to lead them.

There are many things that can be taught and practised in such groups that may be difficult in the normal children's ministry programme. Sometimes these might be all-age activities, but they need not necessarily be so. There may be benefit from having a father/son or mother/daughter workshop day, or even mixing the genders, but take care that this does not exclude some children.

Just as with an adult programme, workshops may be held over a series of meetings or as a kind of day conference. It depends on the subject and the age range of the children concerned. Workshops may be for a small group of children, because only a few are interested in the topic, or because only a few can have 'hands-on' experience at a time.

The following represent just a few suitable topics for workshops: Prayer; Getting the most from our Bible; Leading worship; Leading a friend to Jesus; The gift of tongues; Making banners; Movement in worship (banners and ribbons or dance); Drama; Using a public address system; Songwriting; Praying for healing; Music for God.

Some children may show an aptitude for the subject of a

workshop. These children may then become part of a ministry group that will develop their knowledge and skills and be enabled to exercise that ministry, either within the children's groups or within the church as a whole.

Recreation

One of the stark factors affecting children today is the lack of freedom. 'Stranger Danger' has led to the sad reality that children have to be escorted everywhere, or at least go in groups. The influence of the world has also led to a sharp contrast between the world's standards and Kingdom standards.

It is also felt by many that childhood itself is under threat, with the pressure on children to grow up quickly. This may be seen by the kind of exposure children have to casual sexual ethics – even if it is promoted as 'safe sex'. Children are plunged into sexual matters they are not emotionally able to cope with. Violence is another trend affecting even young children. Physical violence is seen to be the answer to any problem – even in the junior school playground. Some feel that commerce plays its part, too, with its adult-style clothing even for toddlers.

It is against this background (and other books cover much more detail) that we should consider the Church's role in helping children to be children. If we are considering the nurture of the whole child, it is perhaps necessary for the Church to consider how to improve the quality of life of its children, especially in the area of recreation. This would seem to be more necessary in some areas than others, but recreation and safe play should be an element in all children's ministry, even if it is merely an occasional 'play day'. Children should be able to see that God approves of their playtime, as well as their worship, prayer and Bible reading. They should be encouraged to play where Kingdom values matter, learning a healthy competitiveness that seeks to give pleasure to others and not just grasp it for oneself. Children can learn about fairness, about rules and how to tackle frustration at not winning, or not being chosen because we are 'no good', by learning that each of us has value and we need to affirm each other. Rather than initiating another gathering, investigate the possibilities of encouraging existing activities.

What are the recreational needs of children in your area?

What action can you take to plead for all children, not just those in the Church?

What can you offer for Christian children? Is there such a need in your church? If so, what steps can you take to meet it?

Holidays and camps

It is readily acknowledged that a church grows when it is able to spend time away together. Away from the home environment, church members can relax together, and develop relationships in a way that seems otherwise impossible. The same can be said for children, although many of them may already know each other fairly well if they belong to the same school.

I have three serious suggestions to make on this subject.

First, when the church goes away, if possible regard it as a conference as much for the children as the adults. As an itinerant children's worker, I am often invited to 'come and do the children's work' for a parish weekend. Most times I reluctantly decline the invitation, because few or none of the existing children's ministry team wish to work with the children. Understandably, if the church has got a top speaker, those members of the fellowship also want to benefit from his/her teaching. However, from my point of view it means that the 'home team' cannot easily build on what I may achieve with the children. The danger is that I become a 'religious child-minder', whose main function is to look after the children and enable the parents to attend the teaching sessions. The fact that I teach the children about Jesus and that we have some great singing is a kind of bonus, but it will be a case of 'back to usual' next week.

I also wonder what children make of the affair, when they hear frequent requests for volunteers to 'help with the children'. Do they feel that no one wants to look after them, that they are really in the way? I wonder if it changes their expectations of the weekend, whether they look on it as a kind of holiday. In many cases, I believe that may be right, and the church ought to employ some kind of reputable entertainers to do a proper job of entertaining them (at a price).

The alternative, of course, is to say from the beginning that this is as much a conference for the children as for the adults. This means that the children's work team will be on duty, finding the fruit of this kind of opportunity to get to know the children, and the kind of openness that develops to each other and to the Holy Spirit. I establish a theme for the children's conference, possibly linked with the adult theme, but not necessarily so. It is a good idea to hire a button-badge machine, and get someone to design a special logo for the event, printing it simply from a computer. I decide a programme to work in conjunction with what the adults are doing, but probably increasing the variety of activity to include craft and games sessions. As with the adults, I recognise that the Spirit of Jesus seems to be able to touch children in a special way at such a time, and I take every opportunity to give children the chance to respond to what they feel Jesus is saying to them.

My second suggestion is to take the children away, all together or in small groups, to the various camps that are held nationally. There is the added advantage at such events of meeting children from different church backgrounds and experiences. This can only serve to enrich the children and help them to think through various issues that otherwise might not seem relevant. Although not all such camps are concerned with children experiencing the power of the Holy Spirit in the way I discuss in this book, that need not rule them out. There are still many things to gain.

The third suggestion is to take the children away, again in small groups or all together, but this time to a camp or 'houseparty' organised by, or for, yourselves alone. There are many suitable venues for such an event, and local enquiries will produce some addresses and phone numbers. I would not recommend taking under-eights unless accompanied by a parent, and I would try to ensure a good leader/child ratio. Again, this should be staffed by the normal children's ministry team as far as possible, though it is often a good idea to get a visiting speaker or team in for all, or part, of the programme. The matter of catering is an economic factor, though those doing the cooking must be extra to the small-group leadership. I recommend that children have some simple chores to do daily. Not only is this good training for Christian service, it often provides excellent opportunities to chat informally with the children. As with craft activities, children will often talk about what they are learning (or misunderstanding) while busy doing something else. The conclusion of such an event might be to invite the parents who are picking the children up to join in some kind of all-age celebration.

As well as the spiritual benefits which will be taken back home, it is a good idea to take a pictorial record, either by a camcorder or photographs, in order to share what you did with the rest of the church family.

School

Our children spend most of their waking hours at school, and some children's workers feel that they are subjected to all kinds of spiritual attack in the process. The school also represents one of the greatest opportunities for outreach and what is termed 'pre-evangelism'. I have three more suggestions: first, that each school should have a group of Christian adults (not just parents) who will commit themselves to pray for the well-being of the school, and for the safety (spiritual and otherwise) of all its children. This can be done in co-operation with the staff, when they realise that this isn't some kind of covert plot. Discretion will be needed about this, of course.

Second, children may be encouraged to form some kind of voluntary Christian group, either at lunchtime or after school. This would be for two purposes: to encourage the Christian children in the school, especially those whose family circumstances do not allow them to attend the usual children's groups at the church; and also to be an evangelistic meeting, run by children for children. There are Christian organisations (e.g. Scripture Union) which have had much experience in this area, and which will be glad to offer advice.

Third, from a pre-evangelistic point of view, a church would do well to form a team of available people who are able to prepare and present an attractive school assembly at least once a term. Such a service will be generally appreciated by head teacher and staff alike, and may even produce fruit among them. This point is made in *All God's Children?*, speaking of the opportunities that arise from the implementation of the 1988 Education Reform Act.[1] Although this activity may not have much to do with children in renewal, the positive contact made by such a team over the years may prove to be of great significance in the process of a child coming to Jesus, and experiencing that power of the Holy Spirit. It is part of the heavy investment in children that may only have long-term results, but which is part of our duty to this very special group of people.

13

Caring for the whole child

Nature shows us that when living things are born, some are very soon able to fend for themselves, while others have to be nurtured for weeks, months, and, in the case of humans, years. There are many reasons for this variety, though it is inevitably linked to the probabilities of survival. If there are many predators, or a huge demand for the same sources of food, then often many offspring are born to compensate for the high percentage of expected loss. In cases where the number of offspring in a birth is likely to be small, much more is invested in the nurture, to enable survival.

What of the new Christian, and in particular, the Christian child? What are the chances of survival of this growing faith? It appears that there is no one answer, for survival depends on so many factors – home environment, school, peers, teaching, pastoral care, fellowship, culture, etc. However, it is clear that all Christians do need careful nurture, and that includes Christian children. As we have seen in an earlier chapter, however, it seems that the Church has generally invested more of its resources in adults, probably on the basis that if parents are properly discipled, then they will train their child/children, as was expected of parents in the Old Testament (Prov. 22:6). However, while this has generally been the right strategy, the Church has often failed to respond to the changes in family life. Our expectations are based on a kind of family life that is no longer so common, even within the Church.

The high cost of living means that both parents are normally working (where there is employment), and so there is less 'family time'. On a recent radio programme examining the demise of table manners, it was said statistics showed that very few families even sit down together for a meal, and from personal research, I find this is also true in many Christian families. It is also true that most parents – especially fathers – feel unable to teach their children about Christ. If this is true of Christian parents, what about the plight of the child of non-Christian parents?

I have already mentioned the responsibility of parents, and the need for the Church to support them in their role, whether or not they are church members. I am underlining the fact that the Church must give a positive lead in the nurture of her children, with a holistic caring that is concerned not just with the soul, but with the body, the mind, the emotions and everything that makes up a child of God.

Pastoring children

Discipleship indicates a pastoral role, yet this is rarely mentioned in connection with children's ministry. Those who work with children are referred to as leaders, teachers, workers, but seldom pastors. Occasionally a church will have a 'Youth Pastor', but it is rare to find them actually pastoring children, because of the parental responsibility.

Do the terms we use to describe our role with children (teacher, leader, etc.) affect or limit what we do?

Which is more important, to teach or to pastor? Why?

The pastoring of children is important, but who should do it? Does this require specific gifting or training? I suggest that the ideal role of the small-group leader is to include the pastoring of the group. This may require a level of commitment that is beyond many small-group leaders, and it may be a long-term goal. The process may be helped by adopting the risky pattern suggested in an earlier chapter, that of seeking to teach less but do more. As far as gifting or training goes, I do believe that some are 'natural' pastors, but it is a gift that can learnt. Certainly it is a spiritual role, and thus I suggest should be given by prayer and the laying-on of hands by the church leadership in some way. (I also believe that each ministry in the church and children's groups should receive such a delegation of authority by the minister, priest or pastor.)

The pastoral relationship is a relationship! It requires the pastor to know his/her 'sheep', and be known by them. This is very difficult if contact with the children is limited to one hour or less each week, and/or there is a rota system of leaders in the children's work. It is probably helpful to keep (confidential) notes on each child as an aide-mémoir. Be sensitive about this. There is a lot of suspicion about the keeping of confidential information and 'big brother' tactics! However, this is merely a means to an end, and that is to get to know a child, his/her birthday, hobbies, school, musical tastes, dreams, fears, etc. When a child feels known, it does a lot for his/her self-esteem – the same is true for adults!

Ministering to children

It is clear that as we begin to pastor children, and minister to them to receive gifts from the Lord the Spirit, we should pay attention as to how we minister. Generally speaking, I believe it is preferable for children to have someone they know praying with them. As has been mentioned previously, do parents know their children may receive prayer ministry, and have they given their approval? I believe they should have the opportunity to be present whenever it happens, though they may need to be asked to be just an observer, rather than a participant. Some children may not feel so free when a parent is nearby.

Here are some simple practicalities:

- Get to their eye level.
- Remember – use simple language and not much of it – no long prayers.
- Don't be afraid of silence, but explain, if the child does not know why you are being so quiet.
- Be gentle with your tone of voice, without being patronising. Respect the worth and dignity of this little brother or sister in Christ.
- Be gentle with your touch. Be careful about misunderstanding – some children have been the victims of child abuse and touch is fearful to them. Ask permission, rather than presuming. Actual contact is not essential.
- Respect confidentiality. If there is an answer to prayer, ask for permission to share it.
- Some children may need help to explain what God has been doing. Be careful not to put words into their mouth, however, in your keenness to have 'success'. God may not have been doing what you thought He was!

Giving and receiving such ministry should be part of 'normal' Christianity. As well as seeing the effects now, we are also affecting the shape of the future Church, when these children are leaders and council members. This being the case, we should continue to have a long time-scale in mind as we seek to help children grow in faith.

In the Bible, faith is always linked with obedience. For

instance, Jesus said, 'If you love me, you will obey what I command ... Whoever has my commands and obeys them, he is the one who loves me' (John 14:15,21).

'The only thing that counts is faith expressing itself through love' (Gal. 5:6).

'... Faith by itself, if it is not accompanied by action, is dead' (Jas. 2:17).

We are seeking to nurture young Christian disciples. Develop the apprenticeship model wherever it can be practised, partnering the children as you exercise your ministry. For instance, let the children see prayer ministry taking place (keep their eyes open), encouraging them to join in. Children naturally learn how to do things by imitation, including prayer ministry (and any other ministry, for that matter!). We are training them in ministry, but they naturally often know how to speak and act with other children in a ministry situation. By contrast, many adults cannot cope with children ministering to them. It may be that the problem is too complex to explain, or too intimate. Children need to respect this, and adults must be allowed to opt for ministry from adults. If children can be integrated into the regular ministry team(s) in your church, ensure they are always in some kind of partnership with an adult. This does not mean that the adult leads, or is even physically present as the children minister. Rather, the adult role is to 'cover' the children with spiritual authority, to give advice and to train without being too intrusive. However, we must be slow to jump in with our corrections and desire to get the theology or wording right. Let it come out in post-mortem discussion.

Exciting times

God is raising up His army of children, but they need us. They need us to prepare ourselves now for what God is going to do, and they will still need us when all kinds of strange and glorious things are happening through the sovereign power of Almighty God. I do not believe we have seen anything like the revival that is imminent. I believe there will be much heart-searching and consternation, even greater than those raised by the manifestations of the Toronto Blessing. There will be many, as there are now, who question whether God would give so much responsibility to children and young people who are so immature. Do they forget that the Lord Jesus Christ invested the future of the Church in the hands of eleven unlikely young men after His ascension?

I have tried to write a practical book that will encourage you to implement the things I have written. I acknowledge that there are many lessons I still have to learn and that there are still many mistakes I will make. I find this path a lonely one at times, for there is little tidiness about this work with children, and people generally want things neat and orderly in the Church. But the Spirit of God is more like the autumn winds, scattering the tidy heaps of leaves so painstakingly gathered. I know there is no turning back, and I must go where the wind blows, even if sometimes it is uncomfortable and demanding.

Jesus says, 'Behold, I am coming soon! My reward is with me, and I will give to everyone according to what he has done' (Rev 22:12). We live in exciting times. The world in which our children live is very different to the one in which we were children. Sometimes I despair about the world and the signs of its godlessness, yet I praise God that I am alive at this point of history. I praise Him because of the exciting advances in all branches of technology that continue to make our world a wonderful place. Most of all, however, I praise Him because of what He is doing in the Church, and especially in and through children.

Notes

Chapter 1

1. Dian Layton, *Soldiers with Little Feet*, 1989 (Shippensberg, USA: Destiny Image Publishers), p. 3.
2. Organised by Anglican Renewal Ministries in September 1992.
3. Second Prophecy, 1978 International Conference for Spiritual Renewal, Canterbury.
4. *Prophecy Today*, vol. 6, no. 1.

Chapter 2

1. *All God's Children?*, 1991 (London: National Society/ Church House Publishing), 1.2.
2. *All God's Children?* 1.8, 1.15.
3. Chris and John Leach, *And For Your Children*, 1994 (Crowborough: Monarch), p. 54.
4. *All God's Children?*, 1.17.
5. *Children in the Way*, 1988 (London: National Society/ Church House Publishing), p. 3.

Chapter 3

1. *And For Your Children*, p. 47.
2. *Towards a Charter for Children in the Church*, 1989, The United Reformed Church.

3. ibid.
4. Roger Mitchell, *Children Now*, published by Icthus Christian Fellowship, 107 Stanstead Road, Forest Hill, London SE23 1HH.
5. ibid.
6. *What Makes Churches Grow?* 1979 (London: The Bible Society). Used with permission.
7. ibid., Unit 5/A2.

Chapter 4

1. Mel Tari, *Like a Mighty Wind*, 1973 (Eastbourne: Kingsway), from the Foreword.
2. David Walters, *Kids in Combat*, 1989 (USA: Good News Fellowship Ministries), p. 10.
3. Francis Bridger, *Children Finding Faith*, 1988 (London: Scripture Union), pp. 186–8.
4. Penny Frank, *Children and Evangelism*, 1992 (London: Marshall Pickering), p. 65.
5. *Kids in Combat*, p. 11.
6. *And For Your Children*, p. 71.
7. Howard Snyder, *Community of the King*, USA NP.
8. John Wimber, *Signs and Wonders*, 1985 (Los Angeles, USA: Vineyard Ministries International), section 3.

Chapter 5

1. One such video is *Children in the Anointing*, a promotional video of the ministry of David Walters, available from Good News Fellowship Ministries, 9 Valley Road, Hounsdown, Totton, Southampton SO4 4FP.
2. Holy Trinity Church, Amersham Road, Hazlemere, Bucks. HP15 7PZ.

Chapter 6

1. Alan Price and Keith Barrett, *Young Saints*, 1993 (Derby: Anglican Renewal Ministries/Lynx Communications).
2. *Kids in Combat*, p. 89.

Chapter 7

1. John Prince, *Whose is the Kingdom?*, 1979 (London: Scripture Union), p. 21.
2. R. Hudson-Pope, *To Teach Others Also: a Handbook for Children's Speakers*, 1953 (London: Scripture Union).
3. *Whose is the Kingdom?*, p. 23.
4. John Inchley, *Realities of Childhood*, 1986 (London: Scripture Union), p. 123.
5. *All God's Children?*, 5.8.
6. Ron Buckland, *Children and God*, 1988 (London: Scripture Union), p. 51.
7. ibid., p. 42.
8. Details of these booklets may be obtained from The Teknon Trust, P.O. Box 239, Derby DE22 1XH.
9. Details of the audio Bible-reading cassettes are available from The Bible Society, Stonehill Green, Westlea, Swindon, Wiltshire SN5 7DG. The children's *Journey into Life* video is being produced by Sonrise Productions, Worthing, and should be available in 1996. A children's audio evangelistic 'booklet' is currently being developed. Further details from The Teknon Trust (address above).
10. Paul Butler, *Reaching Children*, 1992 (London: Scripture Union), p. 40.

Chapter 10

1. Eddie Gibbs, *Urban Church Growth: Some Clues from Britain and South America*, 1977 (Nottingham: Grove Books).
2. *All God's Children?* 1.15.
3. Ian Smale, *Angels with Dirty Faces*, 1989 (Eastbourne: Kingsway), p. 118.
4. Details of suppliers of such short length cassettes may be found by studying advertisements in specialist hi-fi magazines available in good newsagents.
5. David Watson, *I Believe in the Church*, 1978 (London: Hodder & Stoughton), p. 179.

Chapter 11

1. Martha Keys Barker, *Building Worship Together*, 1981 (Poole: Celebration Services [Post Green] Ltd.), p. 13.
2. *I Believe in the Church*, p. 184.

Chapter 12

1. *All God's Children?*, 6.8, 6.9, 6.10.

Appendix

Under 5s

- short attention span, so use several different activities and methods of presentation, even if you repeat some of them at different times.
- dependent on adults, so there needs to be a small ratio of helpers to children; 1:6 is the ideal.
- physically small, so always ask yourself if something is too high up for them to see. If so, come down to their level.
- have fears. Don't dismiss these but instead encourage the child and give a lot of assurance. The use of puppets to personalise fears and how to deal with them can be useful, e.g. 'Spider' or a 'Darkness Monster' who can talk and show itself to be nothing to be really afraid of.
- movements often unco-ordinated, so make allowances when using percussion, etc.
- fantasy and fact are equally real. 'Pretend' activities can help them to learn a lot, e.g. 'Let's pretend to be a fisherman in Galilee. Look, here comes Jesus! Put down your net and greet Him . . .', etc.
- may prefer to play alone and may not be able to work with others.
- emotions are swiftly aroused, deep and shortlived. May be very upset at the death of Jesus or equally very excited with the feeding of 5,000 from the boy's loaves and fishes.

- believe what they are told so that Father Christmas, fairies and pixies are as real as Jesus. Try to distinguish between a 'story' and what is real.
- life centred around home and neighbourhood. Illustrations and examples should come from the children's experiences.
- imitate others, including you. Do your actions back up your words?
- want to please so give lots of praise where it is due.
- limited vocabulary and understanding so watch your language! Don't be afraid of using a 'big' word, just make sure they understand what it means.
- literalist. 'Ask Jesus to come into your heart' means to ask Him to come into that pumphouse in our bodies! Ask questions so be ready for them, give time for them; it is a way of participation.

– no sense of time. 'Next week' may as well be 'next year'. Similarly 'thousands of years before Jesus' means little to the under 5s.

5 to 7s

– short attention span.
– growing in independence and more keen to do things without help: colour pictures, cut out shapes, etc. – though 'back up' help is still needed.
– growing in spurts and energetic. Action songs and quick games can harness this energy.
– have fears.
– developing physical skills so can attempt a bigger range of expression work, using scissors, etc.

- imaginative. Use this to help them 'picture' the settings of your stories.
- play with others so expression work like collages can be done in groups.
- co-operative if given good reason. Appeal to their developing logic, e.g. 'Let's all be quiet so that everyone can hear. If someone can't hear they might spoil the story . . .', etc.
- believe what they are told.
- becoming more observant so detail in pictures is more important.
- proud of achievements so need encouragement; rewards for things done and incentives to keep working are important.
- increasing range of vocabulary so your words do not need to be so simple.
- understand words at face value, i.e. literal thinkers.
- inquisitive. A mystery box containing your visual aid can be an attention grabber, building up interest to the time when you can produce its contents.
- concerned with the present. Does your story relate to 'now' or 'then'?
- enjoy learning through repetition so make use of memory verses and short songs.

7 to 10s

- concrete thinkers: love, truth and abstract ideas need to be made concrete – give specific examples.
- increasingly independent. Can be given project work, for instance, and left to carry on if the incentive and interest is there.
- active and energetic. Harness this, rather than suppress it. Use games and action songs that need a lot of energy (if you can stand the pace!).

- love adventure and so adventure stories capture the interest – the Bible is full of them.
- becoming more skilful, e.g. many can play an instrument well and perhaps can contribute to a meeting.
- strong sense of justice: fair play is demanded in quizzes and games.
- friendships are important so beware of splitting up friends unless this is for disciplinary reasons. Also look out for the child with no friends; they can be very lonely.
- curious and usually want to learn. Build up the curiosity factor to stimulate the motivation to learn.
- developing a moral sense and so the practical outworking of being a Christian is quite important.
- hero worship so stories of Bible 'heroes' (Daniel, Joshua, etc.) are very popular. Similarly *you* might become the hero – a situation that can be abused or used profitably.

- enjoy making things, so more ambitious craftwork can be attempted – libraries and schools are full of ideas.
- interested in a wide variety of subjects so be ready for a mine of information on totally irrelevant topics! At the same time remember that listening to details of a child's favourite hobby can be a great way of building a relationship.
- use of language still literalistic. However, because of a developing ability to reason, they can understand concepts and phrases like the well-worn 'asking Jesus into your heart', etc.
- becoming self-aware and self-conscious. We must be very careful not to embarrass.

10 to 13s

- becoming self-critical and sometimes idealistic. Can be negative about themselves because they do not match up to their own image of what they should be like. We need to give much reassurance and try to be confidence builders.
- beginning to grasp abstract ideas so a wider range of biblical truths can be dealt with.
- girls develop faster than boys so having separate groups for girls and boys might be beneficial.
- sensitive to criticism so be careful!
- becoming physically mature yet can tire easily. Make allowances for growth in spurts.
- listen to other points of view and developing views and attitudes. Discussions can be much better than previously.
- becoming sexually curious. We must be positive and honest when the topic occurs, to counter the furtive 'dirty' talk and smutty humour.
- strongly influenced by 'the gang'. A decision for Christ can sometimes be a 'group' decision, i.e. one member will not

make a decision until the rest of the group does. Lesser decisions are of course also made on a group basis.

– sometimes hostile to authority yet they need to know the boundaries, the limits to which they can go before you react.

– more sophisticated in ways of learning so we need to be imaginative in our ways of communication using all available resources: school, diocesan office, etc.

– able to think critically.

– often live by double standards, i.e. peer pressure makes it difficult to relate their Christianity into the world of their friends.

– sometimes moody. We need to make allowances for this and recognise it as part of adolescence.

– influenced by pop music, fashion, football, etc.

Captain Alan Price has been a Church Army evangelist for many years. He now works for The Teknon Trust, seeking to help children and young people to experience more of God's love and purpose for their lives through the power and ministry of the Holy Spirit.

If you would like more information, please contact Alan Price at the address below:

The Teknon Trust
P.O. Box 239
Derby
DE22 1XH
Tel. and fax: 01332 372092